ESSENTIAL TORT

SECOND EDITION

Cavendish
Publishing
Limited

London • Sydney

Titles in the series:

ESSENTIAL TORT

SECOND EDITION

Richard Owen, LLB, LLM, Solicitor
Senior Lecturer in Law
University of Glamorgan Law School

Cavendish
Publishing
Limited

London • Sydney

First published in Great Britain 1994 by Cavendish Publishing
Limited, The Glass House, Wharton Street, London WC1X 9PX

Telephone: 0171-278 8000   Facsimile: 0171-278 8080

E-mail: info@cavendishpublishing.com

Visit our Home Page on http://www.cavendishpublishing.com

Owen, Richard
Essential Tort – 2nd ed
1. Torts – England 2. Torts – Wales
I Title
346.4'2'03

ISBN 1 85941 365 X
Printed and bound in Great Britain

Foreword

This book is part of the Cavendish Essential series. The books in the series are designed to provide useful revision aids for the hard-pressed student. They are not, of course, intended to be substitutes for more detailed treatises. Other textbooks in the Cavendish portfolio must supply these gaps.

The Cavendish Essential Series is now in its second edition and is a well-established favourite among students.

The team of authors bring a wealth of lecturing and examining experience to the task in hand. Many of us can even recall what it was like to face law examinations!

Professor Nicholas Bourne
General Editor, Essential Series
Swansea

Summer 1997

Contents

1 Negligence

You should be familiar with the following areas:

Duty of care

- development of a test for ascertaining the existence of a duty: 'duty situations'; 'two stage' test and 'three stage' test
- policy considerations
- physical injury
- rescuers
- liability for omissions
- nervous shock or psychiatric illness
- economic loss
- negligent mis-statements
- other special relationships
- liability for defective products/buildings
- exercise of statutory powers

Breach of duty: standard of care

- standard of care
- guidelines for assessing standard of care
- standard for skilled defendants
- standard for children/insane/physically ill
- proof of breach: Civil Evidence Act; *res ipsa loquitur*

Causation

- 'but for' test
- successive causes
- multiple causes
- *novus actus interveniens*

Remoteness of damage

- *Re Polemis*
- *Wagon Mound*
- 'Thin skull' rule

Duty of care

Examination questions often concentrate on the historical development of the concept of duty of care and how expressions such as 'proximity' vary in meaning according to when and by whom they are used.

Duty situations

The tests for determining the existence of a duty of care have changed. Prior to 1932 there were numerous incidents of liability for negligence but there was no connecting principle formulated which could be regarded as the basis of all of them. These were referred to as 'duty situations'.

The neighbour principle

The first attempt to create a rationale for all the discrete duty situations was made by Brett MR in *Heaven v Pender* (1883) but the most important formulation of a general principle is that of Lord Atkin in *Donoghue v Stevenson* (1932). This is known as the 'neighbour principle'.

> You must take reasonable care to avoid acts or omissions which you can reasonably foresee are likely to injure your neighbour. Who, then, in law is my neighbour? The answer seems to be – persons who are so closely and directly affected by my act that I ought reasonably to have them in contemplation as being so affected when I am directing my mind to the acts or omissions which are called into question.

The 'two stage' test

The 'neighbour principle' is a test based on reasonable foresight and is unquestionably too wide. It needed further defining.

In the 1970s there were attempts to extend it by defining it as a general principle. In *Home Office v Dorset Yacht Co Ltd* (1970), Lord Reid said '[the neighbour principle] ought to apply unless there is some justification or valid explanation for its exclusion'. This lead to Lord Wilberforce's 'two stage' test in the case of *Anns v Merton LBC* (1977):

> First, one has to ask whether ... there is a sufficient relationship of proximity ... in which case a *prima facie* duty arises. Secondly, if the first question is answered affirmatively, it is necessary to consider whether there are any policy considerations which ought to negative, or to reduce or limit the scope of the duty.

Lord Wilberforce's emphasis on *prima facie* duties lead to a large potential increase in the areas where a duty will be owed, particularly in the area of economic loss. See *Junior Books Ltd v Veitchi Co Ltd* (1983). Note how Lord Wilberforce uses this expression 'proximity', he equates it to foreseeability, this approach has not been followed in more recent cases and 'proximity' currently takes into account the type of situation and policy.

Criticism of the 'two stage' test

Criticisms of the test were as follows:

- policy and proximity are traditionally considered together;
- the test obscured the difference between misfeasance and non-feasance;
- the test involved too rapid an extension to the tort of negligence;
- judges disliked the express consideration of policy.

The 'three stage' test

Lord Wilberforce's general principle soon came in for heavy criticism. This began with Lord Keith in *Governors of the Peabody Donation Fund v Sir Lindsay Parkinson & Co Ltd* (1985) when he said that in addition to proximity the court must decide whether it is 'fair, just and reasonable' to impose a duty of care.

The case of *Murphy v Brentwood DC* (1990) marked the death knell for the 'two stage' test by overruling *Anns. Murphy* talked of adopting an 'incremental' approach, to determining the existence of a duty of care. Following the case of *Caparo Industries plc v Dickman* (1990) there is now a 'three stage' test, with the following criteria being taken into account:

- reasonable foreseeability;
- proximity;
- is it 'fair, just and reasonable' to impose a duty?

The reaction against the 'two stage' test was primarily focused on the fact that it created a massive extension to the tort of negligence. The 'incremental' approach avoids such an increase, instead, the tort of negligence is developed by analogy with existing cases. Any novel type of situation would have to show that it is analogous to an existing situation where a duty is owed.

Policy considerations

Policy plays a vital role in determining the existence of a duty of care. It can be defined as the departure from established legal principle for pragmatic purposes. Cases such as *Donoghue v Stevenson* and *Anns* consider policy expressly, whereas the approach followed in *Caparo* and *Murphy* is to impliedly consider policy and merge it into other considerations such as 'proximity' and whether it is 'fair, just and reasonable' to impose a duty.

What issues of policy are commonly raised?

- To allow an action would open the 'floodgates' and expose the defendant to an indeterminate liability

  The courts are always keen to limit liability to a determinate amount to a determinate class of persons. For example, in *Weller & Co v Foot and Mouth Disease Research Institute* (1986) the plaintiffs were auctioneers who lost money on account of being unable to hold their auctions as a result of the defendant's negligence in allowing the foot and mouth virus to escape, which lead to restrictions on the movement of cattle. It was said by the court that their damage was 'foreseeable' but so was the damage to 'countless other enterprises'. It would have been equally foreseeable that cafés, newsagents etc in the market town would also lose money. The burden on one pair of defendant's shoulders would be insupportable and policy had to act to limit liability.

- The imposition of a duty would prevent the defendant from doing his job properly

  This leads to a class of what have been termed 'protected parties' – persons who enjoy immunity from suit:

  (a) judges and witnesses in judicial proceedings enjoy immunity on grounds of 'public policy';
  (b) barristers – it was held in *Rondel v Worsley* (1969) that barristers were immune from civil action. It was further held in *Saif Ali v Sydney Mitchell and Co* (1980) that the immunity extended to pre-trial work;
  (c) solicitors enjoy immunity when acting as advocates;
  (d) there is a public policy immunity for the carrying out of public duties by public bodies, unless that public body has assumed a responsibility to the individual. It is thought that to impose a

duty, in this situation, would interfere with the way in which public bodies carry out their tasks. The immunity originates with the case of *Hill v Chief Constable of West Yorkshire* (1989). The mother of the last victim of the Yorkshire Ripper sought to sue the police for negligence in failing to apprehend him earlier. There was found to be no special relationship between the police and the victim and consequently no duty could arise. It was felt that to impose a duty would be damaging to police operations. They would deploy their resources defensively on the basis of how they could best avoid civil liability, rather than on the basis of their professional judgment.

This immunity was held to apply in the case of *Osman v Ferguson* (1992), even where it was known to the police that the plaintiff was being harassed by an identified individual. A school teacher had become obsessed with one of his pupils. He had threatened to do a 'thing like the Hungerford massacre' because of the obsession. Complaints had been made by the plaintiff's family to the police. The same individual eventually shot and injured the plaintiff and also killed his father but there was no duty on grounds of public policy immunity.

However, the police may be liable where there is a special relationship between the police and an informant (*Swinney v Chief Constable of Northumbria Police* (1996)). The police do not have a blanket immunity, there are other considerations of public policy which also carry weight. Hirst LJ gave examples such as the need to protect springs of information, to protect informers, and to encourage them to come forward without an undue fear of the risk that their identity will become known to the suspect or to his associates. The facts of the case were that the plaintiff passed on to the police certain information concerning the unlawful killing of a police officer. The suspect was known to be violent. The informant requested that contact with her be made in confidence. The document containing the information supplied together with the informant's name was left in an unattended police car. The vehicle was broken into and the suspect obtained the document. It was arguable that a special relationship existed.

The immunity also did not arise in *Welton v North Cornwall District Council* (1996). An environmental health officer, acting on behalf of a local authority, negligently required the owner of food premises to undertake extensive works to comply with the Food Act 1990. It was argued that the officer exercised a police or quasi-police function and there should be an immunity. This was rejected as the officer had assumed responsibility and hence a duty of care was owed.

The same public policy immunity for the discharge of public duties, unless responsibility had exceptionally been assumed to a particular defendant, also applies to the Crown Prosecution Service (*Elguzouli-Daf v Commissioner of Police of the Metropolis* (1994)) and the fire brigade (*Church of Jesus Christ of Latter Day Saints (Great Britain) v Yorkshire Fire and Civil Defence Authority* (1996); *John Munroe (Acrylics) Ltd v London Fire and Civil Defence Authority* (1996); *Nelson Holdings Ltd v British Gas plc* (1996)). However, a distinction was made between a positive act of negligence for which there would be liability on the part of the fire brigade and a negligent omission for which there would be no liability in *Capital Counties plc v Hampshire County Council* (1997). *Latter Days Saints* and *Munroe* were preferred in *Nelson*.

The public policy immunities have recently been scrutinised by the European Commission of Human Rights. In a reference by the plaintiff in the *Osman v Ferguson* case the Commission found there had been a breach of Article 2 of the European Convention on Human Rights. This protects the right to life and the police were under an obligation to protect the life of Mr Osman and his son.

- It is against public policy to claim that you should not have been born (*McKay v Essex Area Health Authority* (1982))
- The courts will not impose a duty where there is an alternative system of compensation (*Hill v Chief Constable of West Yorkshire*) where compensation was payable under the Criminal Injuries Compensation Scheme
- Constitutional relationship between Parliament and the courts

The courts are reluctant to impose a duty where none existed before, as they see this as the constitutional role of Parliament.

Duty in fact

The issue of the existence of a duty will only arise in novel cases or where it is sought to overrule an existing precedent against liability. This is referred to as a 'notional duty' and looks at the question from an abstracted level.

In most cases, it will be a question of fact, whether the defendant owes the plaintiff a duty of care on the particular facts of the case. This is referred to as a 'duty in fact'. The existence of that particular duty is not in issue, what is in issue is whether a duty is owed in that particular case. For example, *Bourhill v Young* (1942) where it was held that the plaintiff was not foreseeable.

Particular aspects of the duty of care

Physical injury

The meaning of the term proximity varies according to who is using the term, when it is being used and the type of injury that has been suffered. As far as physical injury is concerned the courts will readily hold the parties to be proximate and for this type of injury proximity really equates to foreseeability. In examination questions where the problem revolves around physical injury it is unlikely that the examiner is requiring detailed consideration of the tests required for a duty of care but the problem will revolve around some other aspect of negligence.

However, the House of Lords has held in *Marc Rich & Co AG v Bishop Rock Marine Co Ltd* (1995) that even in cases of physical damage the court had to consider not only foreseeability and proximity but also whether it was fair, just and reasonable to impose a duty.

The third requirement of 'fair, just and reasonableness' was lacking in *Mulcahy v Ministry of Defence* (1996). The plaintiff was a soldier serving with the British army in the Gulf War. He was injured and his hearing was affected when his gun commander negligently ordered a gun to be fired. Two of the components of a duty of care – foreseeability and proximity – were found to be present. However, taking into account the circumstances including the position and role of the alleged tortfeasor and relevant policy considerations, it was not fair, just and reasonable to impose a duty.

An unusual case of negligence causing physical injury is *Revill v Newberry* (1995). The plaintiff, who was a trespasser and engaged in criminal activities was attempting to break into a brick shed on the defendant's allotment. The defendant poked a shotgun through a small hole in the door and fired, injuring the plaintiff. The defendant was found to be negligent and had exceeded the level of violence justified in self-defence. The plaintiff, however, was found to be two-thirds contributorily negligent.

Rescuers

Rescuers as plaintiff

The law does not oblige a person to undertake a rescue, unless they are in a special relationship, but the courts are favourably disposed to someone who does attempt a rescue and is injured in the process. Like physical injury the courts require very little more than foreseeability before they hold the parties proximate.

The courts have held that where the defendant has negligently created a situation of danger, it is foreseeable that someone will attempt a rescue and it will not be possible for the defendant to argue that the rescuer is *volenti non fit injuria* or constitutes a *novus actus interveniens* (*Haynes v Harwood* (1935)); *Baker v TE Hopkins & Son Ltd* (1958)).

As far as rescuers are concerned, the courts are quick to regard someone as being foreseeable and impose few conditions in declaring the parties proximate. However, there must be a real threat of danger (*Cutler v United Dairies (London) Ltd* (1983)). The plaintiff attempted a rescue when no one was in a situation of danger and was consequently not owed a duty.

However, even if the victim was not in actual danger, the defendant will owe a duty if the rescuer's perception of danger was a reasonable one (*Ould v Butler's Wharf Ltd* (1953)).

The duty owed to a rescuer is independent from that owed to the accident victim. The defendant may, therefore, owe a duty to the rescuer where none is owed to the accident victim (*Videan v British Transport Commission* (1963)).

If someone negligently imperils himself or his property, it is foreseeable that there may be an attempt at a rescue and a duty of care will arise on the part of the accident victim. This includes a duty of care to a professional rescuer, such as a fireman (*Ogwo v Taylor* (1987)).

Professional rescuers were also the subject of *Frost v Chief Constable of South Yorkshire Police* (1996). The case arose out of the Hillsborough disaster. The plaintiffs were police officers, four of whom were at the ground at the time of the tragedy, but their roles differed. Three of the four were found to be rescuers. A fifth officer who was not on duty at the ground but reported to a hospital later in the afternoon and helped in mortuary duties was not found to be a rescuer and her claim was dismissed. All five officers had suffered post-traumatic stress disorder and claimed in nervous shock. The claims of civilian relatives of victims for nervous shock damages had been dismissed in *Alcock v Chief Constable of South Yorkshire* (1992). Despite the fact that both cases arise out of the same incident, the four officers who were present at the ground succeeded in *Frost*. The three officers who were classed as rescuers were owed a duty in two capacities. In their first capacity as rescuers and in their second capacity as employees of the defendant. The fourth officer present at the ground was owed a duty as he was the defendant's employee.

Rescuers as defendant

Although rescuers are quickly held to be owed a duty, there are situations where a rescuer himself can owe a duty to the accident victim. For example, where the rescuer by his conduct in commencing a rescue deters or prevents others from attempting a rescue, on the principle of 'detrimental reliance' (*Zelenko v Gimbel Bros* (1935)). There is Canadian authority for saying that where a rescuer worsens the condition of the accident victim, then the rescuer becomes liable to the accident victim (*Horsley v MacLaren* (1970)).

Contributory negligence and rescuers

The courts are reluctant to hold rescuers contributorily negligent, for example, *Harrison v BRB* (1981) but if a rescuer has been contributorily negligent damages will be reduced accordingly (*Sayers v Harlow UDC* (1958)).

Omissions

The law makes a distinction between misfeasance and nonfeasance. There is liability for the former but not for the latter. In other words, there is no liability for omissions. A can watch B drown in an inch of water and incur no legal liability, unless A stands in a special relationship to B. However, if you start off a chain of events and then omit to do something, eg begin driving a car and then omit to brake, with the result that you knock someone down, then there will be liability.

Liability for acts of third parties

Similarly, you cannot be held liable for the acts of third parties, unless there is a special relationship with that third party. In *P Perl (Exporters) Ltd v Camden LBC* (1984), thieves gained entry into the defendant's flat and were then able to break into the plaintiff's property. It was accepted that the damage was foreseeable but there was no obligation on the part of the defendants to prevent the harm from occurring. *Perl* was followed in the case of *King v Liverpool City Council* (1986). In this case, the defendants left their property vacant and unprotected, with the result that vandals gained entrance, damaging the plaintiff's flat. The defendants were held not to be responsible for the acts of the vandals. What particularly troubled the court was the question of what would be the extent of the defendant's obligation, if he was obliged to protect his property. Would it have to be put under 24 hour guard? etc.

In *Smith v Littlewoods Organisation Ltd* (1987), it was held that the defendant could be responsible for the acts of third parties if 'special circumstances' existed, as follows:

- a 'special relationship' between plaintiff and defendant;
- a source of danger was negligently created by the defendant and it was reasonably foreseeable that third parties would interfere;
- the defendant had a knowledge or means of knowledge that a third party had created or was creating a risk of danger on his property and failed to take reasonable steps to abate it.

On the facts of *Littlewoods*, the damage was not reasonably foreseeable, so the defendants were not liable. There was a difference in approach between the judges. Lord Goff saw the intervention of a third party as a *novus actus interveniens* which 'breaks the chain of causation'. Lord Mackay, on the other hand, did not see the question in terms of remoteness and causation but in terms of fault. He felt that a third party intervention does not absolve the defendant from liability but in most cases the chances of harm being caused by a third party are slim, therefore, it is not reasonable to expect the defendant to take precautions against the harm occurring.

Lord Goff's view is preferred by most academic writers and was followed by the Court of Appeal in *Topp v London Country Buses (South West) Ltd* (1993). An employee of the defendant bus company habitually left his bus unlocked with the key in the ignition. After a short interval, a relief driver would drive the bus away. On the day in question, the relief driver failed to turn up and some time later the bus was stolen by joy riders who knocked down and killed the plaintiff's wife. The Court of Appeal held that no duty of care arose. Arguably, if Lord Mackay's test had been used, then the plaintiff would have succeeded as the trial judge had found the defendant's actions to be careless.

Nervous shock or psychiatric injury

The courts have been slow to allow claims for nervous shock unless they are coupled with physical injury to the plaintiff. There are many criteria that the plaintiff must satisfy before there is liability for nervous shock.

Primary victims

The law of negligence relating to nervous shock makes an important distinction between primary and secondary victims. Primary victims are those who have been directly involved in the accident and are within the range of foreseeable physical injury. In the case of secondary victims who are not within the range foreseeable physical injury, certain control mechanisms are put in place to limit the number of claimants to avoid an opening of the floodgates. These principles are derived from a decision by the House of Lords in *Page v Smith* (1995). The plaintiff suffered from *myalgic encephalomyelitis*, also known as chronic fatigue syndrome or post viral fatigue syndrome. In the eyes of the law, this is regarded as a psychiatric injury. The plaintiff was physically uninjured in a collision between his car and a car driven by the defendant but his condition became chronic and permanent, as a result of the accident. Secondary victims are required to show that injury by way of nervous shock had to be foreseeable (*Bourhill v Young* (1943); *King v Phillips* (1953)).

In *Page v Smith*, the collision was relatively minor and nervous shock was not foreseeable. Nevertheless, the plaintiff recovered as a result of the foreseeability of physical injury, even though the plaintiff was not actually physically injured. Lord Lloyd felt that to enquire whether the plaintiff was actually physically injured introduces hindsight into the question of foreseeability, which has no part to play with primary victims. However, hindsight was a legitimate consideration with secondary victims. Lord Lloyd also felt that there was no justification for introducing a distinction between physical and psychiatric illness, at least as far as primary victims are concerned.

Lord Keith, in a dissenting judgment, felt that the injury had to belong to a class or character that was foreseeable.

Rescuers and employees were classed as primary victims in *Frost v Chief Constable of South Yorkshire* (1996), although Judge LJ dissented from this view and it was not considered in *Page v Smith*.

Distinction between primary and secondary victims

Primary victims	Secondary victims
No policy control mechanisms to limit the number of claimants	Policy control mechanisms to limit claimants
Foreseeability of physical injury	Foreseeability of injury by way of nervous shock
Issue of foreseeability considered prospectively	Issue of foreseeability considered with hindsight
No distinction between physical or psychiatric injury	Distinction between physical and psychiatric injury. Foreseeability judged by reference to whether a person of normal fortitude would have suffered a recognisable illness

Secondary victims

Medically recognised psychiatric illness or disorder

Before there can be liability for secondary victims there must be a medically recognised psychiatric illness or medical disorder, there is no liability for emotional distress or grief unless this leads to a recognisable medical condition these have been held to include:

- depression (*Chadwick v British Transport Commission* (1967));
- personality change (*McLoughlin v O'Brian* (1983));
- post-traumatic stress disorder (*Hale v London Underground* (1992)).

It was held in *Hicks v Chief Constable of South Yorkshire* (1992) that there could be no claim for the terror suffered immediately before death for the knowledge that death was imminent. An abnormally sensitive plaintiff will be unable to recover unless a person of 'normal' fortitude would have suffered.

The distinction between grief and a recognised psychiatric condition was again discussed in *Vernon v Bosley (No 1)* (1996). The plaintiff was found to suffer from post-traumatic stress disorder (PTSD), complicated by a grief reaction. While PTSD is recoverable because it is a recognised psychiatric condition, grief is not compensatable. It was held by a majority that although the rules of nervous shock limit the number of potential claimants, they do not limit the compensation to those who are owed a duty of care. Even though part of the injury was attributable to grief, damages were recoverable in full.

Additional criteria

In addition to the above there are other criteria that the secondary victim will have to satisfy before the plaintiff can recover for nervous shock:

- proximity in terms of relationship – the plaintiff must be in a close and loving relationship with the accident victim (rescuers are an exception to this rule);
- proximity in terms of time and space – the plaintiff must be at the scene of the accident, in the vicinity of the accident or have come across the 'immediate aftermath' of the accident;
- reasonable foreseeability – the plaintiff's injuries must have been reasonably foreseeable;
- there must have been a direct perception of the accident by the plaintiff with the plaintiff's own 'unaided senses';
- sudden shock – the illness must have been caused by a sudden shock.

Proximity in terms of relationship

Own safety

Initially, the law only allowed recovery where the plaintiff had been put in fear of his own safety (*Dulieu v White* (1901)). Note the rules which now relate to primary victims, *Page v Smith* above. The plaintiff in *McFarlane v EE Caledonia Ltd* (1994) was on a support vessel at the *Piper Alpha* disaster. At first instance, it was held that he could recover even though he was not a person of reasonable fortitude, as he had feared for his own safety. This was overturned by the Court of Appeal. Stuart-Smith LJ said that to claim for your own safety the plaintiff would have to be:

- in the actual area of danger;
- while not in the area of actual danger, because of the sudden and unexpected nature of the event, the plaintiff reasonably thinks he is;
- while not originally in the area of danger, the plaintiff is involved later, ie a rescuer.

In *McFarlane v Wilkinson* (1997), the plaintiff was on a vessel close to the *Piper Alpha* disaster but could not be classed as a primary victim. The vessel was close to danger but never actually in danger.

Fear for the safety of others

Eventually the law was extended so that recovery was allowed where the plaintiff feared for the safety of others. *Hambrook v Stokes* (1925) is authority for this proposition, although it should be noted that this is a difficult case and evidence was adduced that the plaintiff had feared for her own safety.

Close and loving relationship

In *Alcock v Chief Constable of South Yorkshire* (1991), it was held by the House of Lords that the plaintiff had to be in a 'close and loving relationship' with the accident victim. This approach rejected an earlier approach by the Court of Appeal which tried to put a restriction on the amount of claims by limiting claimants to specific categories, such as parents and spouses.

Nervous shock caused through damage to property

The cases looked at so far have concentrated on nervous shock following the negligent infliction of personal injury on a loved one. Claims have been allowed for damage to property as well as physical injury. The Court of Appeal in *Attia v British Gas* (1988) allowed for nervous shock after the plaintiff witnessed her house burning down as a result of the defendant's negligence in installing central heating.

Rescuers

Rescuers are an exception to the rule that claimants for nervous shock have to be in a 'close and loving relationship' with the accident victim. In *Chadwick v British Railways Board* (1967), the plaintiff was a passer-by who assisted at the scene of a rail disaster. He did not know the accident victims but was able to recover. In *Hale v London Underground* (1992), a professional rescuer, a fireman, was awarded damages for nervous shock.

Professional rescuers were again allowed to recover in *Frost v Chief Constable of South Yorkshire* (1996). The case was another Hillsborough stadium disaster case. The five plaintiffs were police officers, four of whom were present at the ground and the fifth discharged mortuary duties at a local hospital following the disaster. Three out of the five plaintiffs were classed as rescuers and were able to recover damages for their psychiatric injuries, on that basis. In addition, as the disaster was caused by the negligence of their employer the four officers present at the ground were owed duties in their capacity as employees from their employer. They were at the scene as a matter of obligation. The fifth officer was not owed a duty as she was neither a rescuer nor at the ground when the negligence occurred. A majority of the Court of Appeal held that rescuers and employees are primary and not secondary victims. This explains the discrepancy between this case and *Alcock*, where relatives of the victims of the disaster did not succeed as they lacked sufficient proximity. *Frost* can also be distinguished from *McFarlane v EE Caledonia Ltd*, as in the latter case the employee was off duty and consequently not owed a duty by his employer, he was not under an obligation to be at the scene of the *Piper Alpha* disaster.

Judge LJ, in a dissenting judgment, held that all employees and all rescuers could not be classed in fixed categories as primary and secondary victims. The classification should depend on the facts of the case.

Proximity in terms of time and space

Initially, the plaintiff had to be at the scene of the accident to be able to recover for nervous shock. In *Bourhill v Young* (1943), the plaintiff was 50 yards from the scene of the accident which she could hear but could not see and was held to be insufficiently proximate. Similarly, in *King v Phillips* (1953), the defendant was a taxi driver who negligently ran over a boy's tricycle. The plaintiff was the boy's mother who witnessed the accident from a distance of 70 yards. It was held that she was insufficiently proximate to the scene of the accident.

However, a change can be detected in the courts' attitude in the case of *Boardman v Sanderson* (1964) where the plaintiff who again heard but was not present at the scene of the accident was able to recover.

In *McLoughlin v O'Brian* (1981), the plaintiff was two miles from the accident but rushed to the hospital to see her family prior to them receiving medical treatment and was held to be sufficiently proximate. She had come across the 'immediate aftermath' of the accident.

In *Jaensch v Coffey* (1984), the plaintiff who saw her husband in hospital in a serious condition after he had been injured, succeeded in her claim for nervous shock.

Reasonable foreseeability

In *Bourhill v Young*, the plaintiff did not recover as she was not regarded as being reasonably foreseeable. Two views formed as to the true ratio of the case. The first view holds that the defendant must be at the scene of the accident. The second view states that injury by way of psychiatric injury must be foreseeable. The latter view is now taken as the test for foreseeability – the defendant should be able to foresee injury by way of nervous shock.

Direct perception

In *McLoughlin v O'Brian*, certain policy issues came to the fore. Lord Wilberforce felt that there was a need to set some limit on the extent of liability and it was therefore necessary to limit claims where there had been a direct perception of the accident with the plaintiff's own unaided senses. Lord Bridge, however, did not see the necessity of setting such an arbitrary limit on claims.

For several years after *McLoughlin v O'Brian*, there was considerable uncertainty as to the state of the law. In *Hevican v Ruane* (1991), the plaintiff saw his son's dead body some time after he died, without coming across the 'immediate aftermath' of the accident. Similarly, at first instance, in *Ravenscroft v Rederiaktiebolaget* (1991), the claim of a mother who did not come across the 'immediate aftermath' was initially allowed.

Alcock settled the fact that it had to be a direct perception of the accident with the plaintiff's own unaided senses. *Ravenscroft v Rederiaktiebolaget* was, as a result, overturned on appeal.

Sudden shock

There must be a sudden shock. This requirement has been doubted in a dissenting judgment by Sir Thomas Bingham MR in *M v Newham LBC* (1994).

Policy or principle?

The policy limitations on the rights of secondary victims to recover have caused many arbitrary distinctions and much dissatisfaction with the law relating to nervous shock. Why was it possible for the police officers present at the Hillsborough disaster to recover (*Frost*) but not relatives of the victims (*Alcock*)? Why can an employee present at the scene of disaster recover (*Frost*) but not an off duty employee similarly present at the scene of disaster (*McFarlane v EE Caledonia Ltd*)? What is the difference between coming onto the immediate aftermath of the accident (*McLoughlin v O'Brian*) and hearing about the accident and seeing its consequences sometime later (*Ravenscroft v Rederiaktiebolaget*)?

Policy limitations have caused great uncertainty as to the state of the law. They are thought necessary, as without them the floodgates would open. There is evidence to suggest that this assumption is not justified. Legislation in New South Wales allowed a parent or spouse to recover for nervous shock, without the requirement that there be proximity in terms of time and space. No flood of litigation followed. *Murphy* (1995) argues that the three stage test should be replicated throughout negligence. There would be no sharp divergence between the treatment of primary and secondary victims and the same tests would be applied. He argues that the actual result would not differ much from the outcome of the decided authorities, as it would still be harder for those who are currently classed as secondary victims to satisfy the proximity stage of the test.

An alternative is to legislate in this area. The Law Commission in its Consultation Paper No 137 have come to the provisional view that legislation is required but do not think that the whole law on negligently inflicted psychiatric illness could be codified. They also take the view that proximity restrictions of some sort should remain.

Economic loss

The law of negligence does not give the same level of protection to economic interests as it does to physical interests. There are only three types of situations where recovery is allowed in negligence for economic loss:

- economic loss which is consequential upon physical damage;
- negligent mis-statements;
- other special relationships.

Economic loss which is consequential upon physical damage

It is long established that economic loss as a result of physical injury is recoverable not only for the cost of repairing physical damage to people or property but also for 'consequential' loss of earnings or profits during convalescence or repair.

Much stricter controls apply in relation to 'commercial losses'. Recovery was not allowed in *Weller v Foot and Mouth DRI* even though the damage was foreseeable as damage was also foreseeable to 'countless other enterprises'.

In *Spartan Steel & Alloys v Martin & Co (Contractors) Ltd* (1973), the defendant negligently cut off electricity to the defendant's factory. Damages for the cost of molten metal which was thrown away were recoverable, since it was consequential upon physical damage, but loss of profits while electricity was cut off were not recoverable as they were purely commercial profits.

This area was greatly affected by the application of the *Anns* test. In *Junior Books v Veitchi Co Ltd* (1983), recovery was allowed for economic loss in a situation where liability had not been held to exist before. The defendants were sub-contractors and flooring specialists and had been nominated by the plaintiffs who had employed the main contractors. The floor was negligently laid and the plaintiffs claimed loss of profits for the period when the floor had to be re-laid. Applying the *Anns* test it was held that the damage was recoverable. This promised to open up a whole new field of claims for economic loss and *Junior Books* has not been followed in subsequent cases, although it has not been formally overruled. The House of Lords found it particularly significant that the sub-contractors had been nominated by the plaintiffs and it was felt that this was sufficient to create a relationship of 'proximity'.

This has become known as the 'high water' mark of economic loss. The courts have since returned to the traditional test. For example, in *Muirhead v Industrial Tank Specialities Ltd* (1985), the plaintiffs who had suffered loss because their lobsters had been killed due to defective motors on a tank could only recover the cost of the lobsters and repairs to the tank, they could not recover for loss of profits. This case has clear echos of *Spartan Steel*. This trend was confirmed by the case of *Leigh and Sillivan v Aliakmon Shipping* (1986) which again held that it was not possible to recover economic losses arising from negligent misconduct.

Negligent mis-statements
So far we have looked at liability for negligent acts, the situation is very different when it comes to statements which cause economic loss. One difficulty is that statements may be made on an informal occasion and may be passed on without the consent of the speaker.

Special relationship
The major development in this area came in the case of *Hedley Byrne & Co Ltd v Heller & Partners* (1964). The House of Lords held that where there was a 'special relationship' between the maker of a statement and the receiver of a statement then there could be liability for the economic loss caused. In this particular case, there was no liability as there had been a disclaimer attached to the statement, so there had not been a 'voluntary assumption of responsibility'.

The Privy Council in *Mutual Life and Citizens' Assurance Co Ltd v Evatt* (1971) attempted to limit the scope of *Hedley Byrne* by stating that it only applied in respect of advice given in the course of a business and where the defendant made it clear that he was claiming some special skill or competence. However, there was a minority view rejecting this approach.

That attempt has not been followed since and the special relationship has been drawn more liberally. It became clear in *Howard Marine & Dredging Co Ltd v Ogden* (1978) that there had to be *considered* advice which someone would act upon. Liability would not extend to off-the-cuff information. So, in *Esso Petroleum v Mardon* (1976), the defendants were liable even though they were not in the business of giving financial advice but they did have experience and special skill and knowledge compared to the plaintiffs. While in *Henderson v Merrett Syndicates Ltd* (1994) there was liability for advice given under a contract. In *Holt v Payne Skillington* (1995), it was held that the duty under *Hedley Byrne* could be greater than that in contract.

The Privy Council in *Royal Bank Trust Co (Trinidad) Ltd v Pampellone* (1987) made a distinction between passing on information and the giving of advice. In *Chaudry v Prabhakar* (1988), liability was imposed when the statement was made on a social occasion but the defendant had specialist knowledge compared to the plaintiff.

Reliance

There must be reliance on the statement by the plaintiff. Take, for example, *Smith v Eric S Bush* and *Harris v Wyre Forest DC* (1990), two appeals heard together by the House of Lords. In the first case, the plaintiff had applied to a building society for a mortgage and was required to pay for a valuation to be done on the property by the defendants for the building society. It was known by the defendants that the valuation would be shown to the plaintiff and that it would form the basis of her decision as to whether she would buy the property. The valuation contained a disclaimer that the defendants would not be liable in the event of any negligence. Lord Templeman said that the relationship was 'akin to contract' and liability was imposed. In contrast to *Hedley Byrne*, this case was decided after the Unfair Contract Terms Act 1977 and the disclaimer failed the reasonableness test. The statement had been used for the purpose for which it was intended.

In the second case, the valuation had been carried out by the local authority. The valuation had not been shown to the plaintiff and it also contained a disclaimer, the defendants were still found to be liable.

However, it was possible for a firm of estate agents to rely on a disclaimer in property particulars as against the purchaser of a property in *McCullagh v Lane Fox and Partners Ltd* (1995). The purchaser had not, in that case, been reasonably entitled to believe that the estate agent at the time of making the statement was assuming responsibility for it. The inclusion of a disclaimer put the matter beyond doubt, nor did the Unfair Contract Terms Act 1977 preclude the estate agent from relying on the disclaimer.

It was held in *Hemmens v Wilson Browne* (1993) that it could not be reasonable to rely on a statement where a solicitor had advised his client's mistress to obtain independent legal advice before executing a document.

In addition to reliance there must be knowledge by the maker of the statement, that the recipient will rely on the statement to his detriment. Both requirements were satisfied in *Welton v North Cornwall District Council* (1996). An environmental health officer negligently required the owner of food premises to comply with the Food Act 1990, by making unnecessary substantial building works and major alterations to the kitchen. He also threatened to close the business down, if the works were not completed. The officer knew that what he said would be relied on by the plaintiffs without independent inquiry and he visited to inspect and approved the works being carried out. The fact that the relationship arose out of the purported exercise of statutory functions did not give rise to an immunity on the part of the local authority. It was not necessary to consider whether it was fair, just and reasonable to impose a duty, as the case did not involve an incremental extension to the *Hedley Byrne* principle.

Purpose

The courts will take into account the purpose for which the statement was made. In *Caparo Industries plc v Dickman*, the plaintiffs were shareholders in a company and as such, were entitled to annual audited accounts. On the basis of these accounts they launched a take-over bid in the company before discovering that the accounts had been negligently audited and had wrongly shown the company to be profit making. The plaintiffs sued the auditors who were found not to be liable. The annual audited accounts were the fulfilment of a statutory obligation, the purpose of which was to enable the shareholders to take decisions about the management of the company, it was not intended to be the basis of an investment decision.

There have been other cases concerning annual audited accounts such as *Al Saudi Banque v Pixley* (1989) where auditors did not owe a duty to a bank which had advanced money to a company on the basis of annual audited accounts and *Al Nakib Investments v Longcroft* (1990) where accounts were provided to existing shareholders to encourage them to buy additional shares in a rights issue but the plaintiffs used the accounts as the basis of a decision to buy additional shares on the stock market and were consequently held not to be owed a duty.

Similarly, in *Mariola Marine Corporation v Lloyds Register of Shipping (The Morning Watch)* (1990) there was no liability where the survey of a ship had been carried out for the purposes of a health and safety inspection when the results of the survey had been used as the basis of a decision to purchase a ship.

A duty of care was owed by a managing agent to future Lloyds' names in *Aitken v Stewart Wrightson Members Agency Ltd* (1995), even though the managing agent had not acted for those names at the time of the reference.

Inequality of bargaining power

It was suggested in *Morgan Crucible v Hill Samuel* (1991) by Hoffman J that the difference between *Smith v Bush* and *Caparo v Dickman* was that in the former the plaintiff was in a weak financial position and was absolutely dependent on the advice she received from the valuer, whereas in *Caparo* the plaintiff was a large company with access to its own legal and accountancy advice. It was therefore necessary to take into account the extent to which it was reasonable for the plaintiff to rely on the advice. This approach was doubted in the case of *McNaughton Papers Group v Hicks Anderson* (1991) by the Court of Appeal.

Misstatements

In *Spring v Guardian Assurance plc* (1994), it was held by the Court of Appeal that the giver of a reference owed no duty to the subject of a reference. Any claim would be in defamation and the defence of privilege would be available.

This was overruled by the House of Lords when it was held that a reference could be the basis of a claim under *Hedley Byrne*.

Other special relationships

There is also a line of cases that allows recovery for pure economic loss in negligence when the special skills and expertise of a provider of professional services has been relied on by someone other than his client.

In *Ross v Caunters* (1979), a solicitor allowed the spouse of a beneficiary to witness a will. As a result, the gift to the beneficiary lapsed. It was held that the solicitor was liable to the beneficiary, as damage to her could have been foreseen and she belonged to a closed category of persons.

Ross v Caunters was decided during the period of the *Anns* test. It was uncertain after the demise of that test whether this type of economic loss would remain recoverable. It was found to have survived in the House of Lords' decision of *White v Jones* (1995). The facts were that the testator of a will cut his two daughters out of his estate following a quarrel. After a reconciliation with his daughters he sent a letter instructing a firm of solicitors that legacies of £9,000 should be given to each of his two daughters, the plaintiffs. The letter was received on 17 July and nothing was done by the solicitors for a month. On 16 August the firm's managing clerk asked the firm's probate department to draw up a will or codicil incorporating the new legacies. The following day the managing clerk went on holiday and on his return a fortnight later he arranged to see the testator on 17 September. The testator died on 14 September before the new will had been executed.

Lord Goff held that the plaintiffs were owed a duty of care as otherwise there would be a lacuna in the law. The solicitor owes a duty of care to his client and generally owes no duty to a third party. If an extension to the *Hedley Byrne* principle were not allowed, there would be no method of enforcing the contractual right. Those who had a valid claim (the testator and his estate) had suffered no loss. Those who had suffered a loss (the disappointed beneficiaries) would not have a valid claim. Lord Browne Wilkinson found that the situation was analogous to *Hedley Byrne*.

It was held in *Hemmens v Wilson Browne* (1993) that the principle would not extend to an *inter vivos* transaction, as it would always be possible to rectify a mistake.

White v Jones could not be relied on in *Goodwill v British Pregnancy Advisory Service* (1996). A woman who knew that her partner had undergone a vasectomy did not use any form of contraception and subsequently became pregnant. Her partner had been assured by the defendants that the operation had been successful and that future contraception was unnecessary. It was argued that the situation was analogous to *White v Jones*. The plaintiff was not owed a duty as it was not known that the advice would be communicated to the advisee and would be acted upon by her. She belonged to an indeterminate class of women with whom the man could have formed a relationship after the operation.

Some indication of the scope of the duty is provided by *Woodward v Wolferstans* (1997). The plaintiff had purchased a property raising 95% of the purchase price by way of mortgage. The defendants were a firm of solicitors who acted for her father who guaranteed the mortgage. There was no contact between the firm and the plaintiff. After the mortgage fell into arrears, the lender commenced possession proceedings. It was held that the defendants had assumed responsibility for tasks which were known or ought to be known to closely affect the plaintiff's economic well being. This did not extend to explaining the details of the transaction and the implications of the mortgage.

Liability for defective products

Donoghue v Stevenson is the basis at common law for stating that a manufacturer can be liable to the ultimate consumer of a product for defects in its manufacture. This area has been greatly affected by the

Consumer Protection Act 1987, which makes manufacturers strictly liable for defects in their products. The common law rules still retain a residuary significance where property is not in private use, the limitation period under the Act has expired, or for claims under £275.

Nature of the loss

Lord Atkin said that damages were recoverable for defective products in respect of injury to the 'consumer's life or property'. This phrase 'property' has come to mean 'other property'. The plaintiff cannot claim in tort for the product being defective in itself. Any claim for the product being worth less than the plaintiff thought it was worth lies in contract. In *D and F Estates v Church Commissioners* (1988), it was held that a defective product would have to have caused damage to other property or personal injury for the claim to be recoverable in negligence. If a dangerous defect is discovered prior to it causing personal injury or damage to other property then this will not be recoverable.

Liability for defective buildings

Liability of Local Authority

This area clearly illustrates the swing that has taken place in the courts' attitude. There is a long line of decisions beginning with *Dutton v Bognor Regis UDC* (1972) and most famously, *Anns v Merton LBC* where local authorities were held liable to building owners in respect of negligent inspections of foundations leading to damage to the building itself.

The flow of cases in favour of the building owner and against local authorities was reversed by the case of *Peabody Donation Fund v Sir Lindsay Parkinson and Co Ltd* (1984) where it was held that local authorities are not liable to the original building owner since he is the author of his own misfortunes and since he is under an obligation to ensure that his work is carried out properly. This was applied in *Investors in Industry Ltd v South Bedfordshire DC* (1986).

Eventually, of course, *Anns* was overruled by the case of *Murphy v Brentwood DC* when it was held that a local authority's only duty was to take 'reasonable care to prevent injury to safety or health' so economic loss in the form of discovering a latent defect before it causes physical injury is not recoverable by anyone whether a building owner or subsequent owner occupier. Physical injury would still be recoverable in the case of an owner occupier and possibly still a building owner if there are 'exceptional circumstances'. These 'exceptional circumstances' existed in the case of *Richardson v West Lindsay DC* (1990) as the builder had no specialised knowledge and there has been reliance on the local authority's opinion, which was known or ought to have been known to the local authority.

Liability of builder

Although it is now virtually impossible to sue a local authority in respect of failure to discover a defect in plans, it may be possible to sue the builder in negligence. A builder will usually only be liable for latent defects which cause personal injury or damage to other property. In exceptional cases a builder will also be liable for defects which are known to the occupier but where it is unreasonable to expect the occupier to remove the defect and it is reasonable to expect the occupier to run the risk of injury which the defect creates. In *Targett v Torfaen Borough Council* (1992) the plaintiff was the tenant of a council house built by the defendants. He fell down a flight of stairs which had no handrail and was unlit. After a 25% deduction for contributory negligence the defendants were held liable. Even though the plaintiff was aware of the danger it was not reasonable to expect him to provide a handrail nor was it unreasonable for him to use the stairway without a handrail.

Lord Goff in *Henderson v Merrett Syndicates Ltd* (1994) said that a building owner would not normally be able to sue a sub-contractor or supplier if sub-contracted work or materials do not conform to the required standard. There would have to be an assumption of responsibility by the sub-contractor or supplier direct to the building owner under *Headley Byrne* principles.

As far as the building itself is concerned it may be possible to sue the builder for breach of statutory duty for breach of building regulations or to bring an action under s 1 of the Defective Premises Act 1972. The Defective Premises Act 1972 only applies to dwellings which are not part of the NHBC scheme.

Exercise of statutory powers

This area deals with the question whether public authorities exercising statutory powers owe any duty to a private individual suffering loss or injury resulting from an authority's negligence.

There are four main problems in this area:

* many statutory powers confer a discretion as to how and whether the relevant power should be exercised;
* where the alleged negligence is a failure to exercise statutory power the question of liability for omissions is raised in its most obvious form;

- recent case law may require the injured individual to pursue a different and more restrictive procedural remedy from the ordinary action instituted by writ;
- finally, the Court of Appeal held that the statutory framework and remedies for adjudication in claims for social security benefits excluded altogether any common law remedy for negligence.

Now, the problem of whether a duty of care will ever be imposed in respect of the negligent exercise of statutory powers and the problem of liability for failure to exercise a power can be considered together.

In *Home Office v Dorset Yacht Co Ltd*, the damage arose in circumstances that were foreseeable. The Home Office had a wide discretion as to how to run Borstals. If the Home Office was held to owe a duty to private individuals for escaping trainees then the exercise of their discretion might be inhibited. So, Lord Diplock stipulated that the Home Office could not be held liable unless the act resulted in an *ultra vires* act of the Home Office or its servants. Borstal officers had disregarded instructions and so their conduct was *ultra vires*. The duty was only owed to those in the immediate vicinity whose property was reasonably foreseeably likely to be damaged or stolen in the immediate escape.

His reasoning was further developed in *Anns v Merton LBC* where the local authority argued that it had merely exercised a power and had not been under a mandatory duty to inspect all foundations. The authority argued that:

- it would not be liable for omitting to inspect; and
- if it was not liable for inspecting it could not be liable for negligent inspection.

Again, it was stated that *ultra vires* conduct could create a duty of care, and that *ultra vires* conduct could be a failure to exercise a power at all, or an improper exercise of that power.

The House of Lords made a distinction between:

- planning/policy decisions; and
- operational decisions,

and stated that they would be far more likely to find a duty of care where there had been an operational error and would be less likely to interfere with policy matters.

Although *Anns* was overruled by *Murphy v Brentwood DC*, it is thought that this policy/operational dichotomy is still valid. It was said in *Rowling v Takaro* (1988) that there was no automatic liability for operational decisions but the distinction could be seen as a preliminary filter. Policy decisions would be automatically filtered out but once this step has been overcome then there is a need to decide whether a duty should be imposed on the basis of foreseeability, proximity and if it was fair, just and reasonable to do so.

As we have already seen, there has been a trend of restricting the tort of negligence in this area. In *Yeun Kun-yeu v AG of Hong Kong* (1987), *Rowling v Takaro Properties* (1988) and *Davis v Radcliffe* (1990). the factors that were cited as militating against a duty of care were similar, eg the distorting effect of potential liability on the decision making process, and the waste of public money involved in civil servants cautiously investigating the case to the detriment of other members of the public, the difficulty of ever proving negligence in the making of such a decision and the difficulty of distinguishing the cases in which legal advice should have been sought.

This generally restrictive approach to negligence claims in this area appears to be a reluctance to introduce the tortious duty of care where there is an existing system of redress or the statutory regulatory system has made no provision for individual claims.

This trend towards the containment of negligence actions can be seen in *Jones v Department of Employment* (1988) where one of the grounds for the Court of Appeal's decision that a social security adjudication officer owed no duty of care to a claimant was that the duty of the adjudication officer lay in the sphere of public law and was only enforceable by way of statutory appeals procedure or by judicial review.

The House of Lords again held that policy decisions were outside the scope of negligence in *X v Bedfordshire County Council* (1995). It was held that where a statutory discretion was imposed on a local authority, it was for the authority to exercise the discretion and nothing which the authority would do within the ambit of the discretion could be actionable at common law.

Where the decision complained of fell outside the statutory discretion, it could give rise to common law liability but where the factors relevant to the exercise of the discretion included matters of policy, the court could not adjudicate on such policy matters and therefore could not reach the decision that it was outside the statutory ambit.

The same conclusion was reached in *Stovin v Wise* (1996) when Lord Hoffman said that the minimum pre-conditions for basing a duty of care on the existence of a statutory power were first, it would have to have been irrational not to have exercised the power, so that there was a public duty to act and secondly, there were exceptional grounds for holding that the policy of the statute required compensation to be paid to persons who suffered loss because the power was not exercised.

Breach of duty: standard of care

Having established that the defendant owes the plaintiff a duty of care, it will next be necessary to determine whether the defendant has in fact breached that duty. The defendant will have fulfilled his duty if he has behaved in accordance with the standard of the reasonable man. This is an objective standard and disregards the personal idiosyncrasies of the defendant. Everyone is judged by the same standard, the only exceptions being skilled defendants, children, the insane and physically ill.

The question whether a person has fulfilled a particular duty is a question of fact. It was held by the House of Lords in *Qualcast (Wolverhampton) Ltd v Haynes* (1959) that reasonableness will depend on the circumstances of the case and it is a mistake to rely on previous cases as precedents for what constitutes negligence. So, in *Worsfold v Howe* (1980), the trial judge held that a driver who had edged out from a side road and across stationary tankers before colliding with a motor-cyclist was negligent as the Court of Appeal had ruled that similar actions were negligent in a previous case. The Court of Appeal held that the previous case laid down no legal principle, that such decisions were to be treated as questions of fact.

Factors of the objective standard

The law provides various guiding principles as to the objective standard.

Reasonable assessment of the risk
This can be further subdivided into two factors.

Degree of likelihood of harm occurring
A reasonable man is not usually expected to take precautions against something where there is only a small risk of it occurring. Two cricketing cases provide a simple illustration. First, in *Bolton v Stone* (1951), a cricket ball had been hit out of a cricket ground six times in 28 years into a nearby, rarely used lane. On the seventh occasion, it hit a passer-by. It was held that the chances of such an accident occurring were so small that it was not reasonable to expect the defendant to take precautions against it happening.

However, in *Miller v Jackson* (1977), a cricket ball was hit out of a ground eight to nine times a season. In this case, it was held that the defendant had been negligent as it was reasonable to expect the defendant to take precautions. The crucial difference between the two cases is that the risk of harm was much greater in this case than in *Bolton v Stone*.

Seriousness of the harm that may occur
This is an exception to the above, as where there is a small risk but the potential harm that may occur is great then a reasonable man would be expected to take precautions.

In *Paris v Stepney BC* (1951), the plaintiff was blind in one eye. While he was working for the defendants a metal chip entered his good eye and rendered him totally blind. The defendants were found to be negligent in failing to supply him with goggles since even though there had only been a small risk, the consequences were serious.

The object to be achieved
The importance of the object to be attained is also a factor which is taken into account when deciding the standard of care. It is necessary to assess the utility of the defendant's act. The greater its social utility, the greater the likelihood of the defendant's behaviour being assessed as reasonable.

In *Watt v Hertfordshire County Council* (1954), the plaintiff was a fireman and part of a rescue team that was rushing to the scene of an accident to rescue a woman trapped under a car. The plaintiff was injured as a heavy piece of equipment, due to the emergency circumstances had not been properly secured on the lorry on which it was travelling. It was held that it was necessary to 'balance the risk against the object to be achieved'. The action for negligence failed as the risk of the equipment causing injury in transit was not so great as to prevent the efforts to save the woman's life.

Practicability of precautions
The cost of avoiding a risk is also a material factor in the standard of care. The defendant will not be expected to spend vast sums of money on avoiding a risk which is very small.

In *Latimer v AEC Ltd* (1953), the defendant's factory was flooded, the water mixed with factory oil and made the floor slippery. Sawdust was spread on the surface but not enough to cover the whole affected area.

It was held that the employers were not negligent. It was necessary to balance the risk against the measures necessary to eliminate it. In this case, the risk was not so great as to justify the expense of closing the factory down.

General and approved practice

If it is shown that the defendant acted in accordance with general and approved practice, then this may be strong evidence that he has not been negligent. However, this is not conclusive and a defendant may still be negligent even though he acted in accordance with a common practice.

There is a obligation on the defendant to keep up to date with developments and to change practices in the light of new knowledge (*Stokes v Guest, Keen and Nettleford (Bolts and Nuts) Ltd* (1968)).

It will not be a defence to say that general and approved practice has been followed, if it is an obvious folly to do so. 'Neglect of duty does not by repetition cease to be neglect of duty' *per* Slesser LJ *Carpenters' Co v British Mutual Banking Co Ltd* (1937).

The doctrine of 'obvious folly' was first expounded by Lord Dunedin in *Morton v William Dixon Ltd* (1907) and a recent illustration can be found in *Re the Herald of Free Enterprise* (1987). Following the *Zeebrugge* ferry disaster the master of the ship claimed that it was general and approved practice for him not to check that the bow doors were closed prior to setting out to sea. It was held that the general and approved practice constituted an 'obvious folly' and should not have been followed.

The general standard and skilled defendants

Skilled defendants are judged by higher standards than the ordinary defendant. The test for skilled defendants was encapsulated by McNair J in *Bolam v Friern Hospital Management Committee* (1957):

> The test is the standard of the ordinary skilled man exercising and professing to have that particular skill. A man need not possess the highest expert skill at the risk of being found negligent. It is well established law that it is sufficient if he exercises the ordinary skill of an ordinary competent man exercising that particular art.

It can be seen that skilled defendants must meet a higher standard than the ordinary person and this is an exception to the rule that everyone is judged by the same standard.

Skilled defendants face a particular problem when trying to invoke the defence of general and approved practice, as often there are conflicting views within a profession as to which course of action is the appropriate course to take. *Bolam* gave an answer to this problem when it stated that a doctor was not negligent if he acted in accordance with a respectable body of opinion merely because another body of opinion took a contrary view. It was also held that a doctor could not be criticised if he believed damages of treatment were minimal and did not stress them to the patient.

Bolam was applied in the case of *Sidaway v Bethlem Royal Hospital Govrs* (1985), where it was held that a doctor was under a duty to inform a patient of special/real risks but this is subject to an overriding duty to act in the patient's best interest.

Trainee experts

The potential harshness of the objective standard for skilled defendants is illustrated by the case of *Wilsher v Essex Area Health Authority* (1988) when it was stated that a young, inexperienced doctor is judged by the standards of a competent experienced doctor even though, by definition, he is unable to attain that standard.

Experts outside the medical field

The same principles extend outside the medical sphere in *Wells v Cooper* (1958) the Court of Appeal held that a householder performing a DIY task was judged by the standard of a reasonably competent carpenter.

In *Philips v William Whiteley* (1938), the court rejected the idea that a jeweller who carried out an ear piercing operation should be judged by the standard of a surgeon but instead the court said that she should be judged by the standard of a reasonably competent jeweller carrying out that particular task.

In *Nettleship v Weston* (1971), a learner driver was judged by the standard of a 'competent and experienced driver' since she held herself out as possessing a certain standard of skill and experience. The court felt that a uniform standard of skill was preferable because of the practical difficulty of assessing a particular person's actual skill or experience.

Expert standard depends on the surrounding circumstances

In the same way as the ordinary standard, the expert standard depends on the circumstances of the particular case.

In *Wooldridge v Sumner* (1963), a momentary lapse on the part of a showjumper did not make him negligent. *Wooldridge v Sumner* involved a participant in a sporting event injuring a spectator. In *Smolden v Whitworth* (1996), it was held that a rugby referee's level of care to a participant in a sporting event was that appropriate in all the circumstances. The threshold of liability was a high one and would not be easily crossed. On the facts of the case, the referee was liable for spinal injuries caused by a collapsed scrum.

Abnormal defendants

Further exceptions to the rule that everyone is judged by the same standard in assessing whether they are negligent are children, the insane and physically ill. Both categories are treated separately and different principles apply.

Children

In *Gough v Thorne* (1966), Lord Denning said that a 12-year-old child could not be contributorily negligent. In *Walmsley v Humenick* (1954), it was held that very young children were incapable of negligence as they were incapable of foreseeing harm. It should be noted that in tort there is no fixed age for liability unlike in criminal law.

A problem with children has been in deciding whether subjective circumstances such as the child's mental ability and maturity be taken into account or should an objective standard be applied in the same way as for adults?

The High Court of Australia in *McHale v Watson* (1966) held that a 12-year-old boy should be judged by 'the foresight and prudence of an ordinary boy of 12'.

The insane and the physically ill

The principles which apply here seem to revolve around whether the defendant was aware of his condition and also whether the defendant had control over his own actions.

Defendant is unaware of the condition

In *Waugh v Allan* (1964), the defendant, a lorry driver, was in the habit of suffering gastric attacks which normally quickly passed. After one such attack, the defendant pulled off the road and when he felt better continued on his journey only to suffer a fatal coronary thrombosis and injured the plaintiff. The defendant was held not to be negligent as he had recovered sufficient skill and judgment to continue his journey.

In *Jones v Dennison* (1971), the defendant was unaware that he suffered from blackout attacks as a result of epilepsy. He suffered a blackout while driving, injuring the plaintiff. It was held that he could not be considered negligent, as he was unaware of his tendency to blackout.

Defendant retains control over his actions

In situations where the defendant retains some control over his actions he will be held liable.

In *Roberts v Ramsbottom* (1980), the defendant suffered a stroke shortly after starting a two and a half mile journey. He had two collisions before colliding with the plaintiff's parked vehicle. It was found that he was aware of the collisions and had retained some impaired control over his actions and consequently was liable.

In *Moriss v Marsden* (1952), the defendant suffered from a mental disease which robbed him of his moral judgment. While suffering from this disease he attacked and injured the plaintiff, while he knew the nature and quality of his act, he did not know that what he was doing was wrong. The defendant was held to be liable.

Proof of breach

The burden of proof rests with the plaintiff on the balance of probabilities. However, there may be ways in which the plaintiff can receive assistance in discharging that burden of proof.

Assistance by statute

Section 11 of the Civil Evidence Act 1968

Where the defendant has been convicted of criminal proceedings that conviction will be admissible in civil proceedings and the defendant will be taken to have committed the acts until the contrary is proved. For example, proof of the defendant's conviction for careless driving places the burden of disproving the occurrence of negligent driving on the defendant.

Assistance at common law

Res ipsa loquitur

'The thing speaks for itself'. This doctrine originally began with the case of *Scott v London and St Katherine's Dock* (1865). First, it should be noted that it is an evidential burden and secondly, three conditions must apply before it can be invoked:

- Accident could not have occurred without negligence

  For example, stones are not found in buns unless someone has been negligent (*Chaproniere v Mason* (1905)); barrels of flour do not fall from warehouse windows onto the street in the absence of negligence (*Byrne v Boadle* (1863)). On the other hand, losses on the commodity market are not *prima facie* evidence of negligence on the part of brokers (*Stafford v Conti Commodity Services Ltd* (1981)); nor is a spark from a domestic fire (*Sochacki v Sas* (1947)).

In *Scott v London and St Katherine's Docks Co*, it was said that the accident must have happened in 'the ordinary course of things'. As a result, the issue has arisen whether the doctrine can apply to matters which are outside the common experience. In *Mahon v Osborne* (1939), a swab had been left inside a patient after an abdominal operation. Scott LJ thought that the doctrine could not apply to surgical operations as they are outside a judge's common experience. Since then the Court of Appeal have allowed the doctrine to be invoked in cases of medical negligence in *Cassidy v Ministry of Health* (1951). Although it was said by Lord Denning in *Hucks v Cole* (1968) that *res ipsa loquitur* could only be invoked against a doctor in 'extreme' cases. This adds to the plaintiff's difficulties in cases of medical negligence which statistically are harder to prove than other types of negligence.

- Control by the defendant

If the defendant is not in control of the situation which could not have occurred without negligence, then the doctrine cannot be invoked.

In *Easson v London & North Eastern Railway Co* (1944) the railway company could not be said to be in control of railway doors on a journey from Edinburgh to London, because of the possibility of interference by a third party.

This can be contrasted with *Gee v Metropolitan Railway Co* (1873) where someone fell trough a train door shortly after it left the station. Here, it could be said to be under the control of the railway company since there was no opportunity for third party interference.

- Absence of alternative explanation by the defendant

The cause of the accident must be unknown (*Barkway v South Western Transport* (1950)).

The effect of the doctrine of res ipsa loquitur

The effect of *res ipsa loquitur* depends principally on the cogency of the inference. The more cogent the inference the greater the defendant's task in overcoming assumptions of negligence. The effect, therefore, is subjective and depends on the case but two views have been formed as to the effect:

- An evidential burden of proof is cast on the defendant

  In other words, the defendant is required to provide a reasonable explanation of how the accident could have occurred without negligence on his part. If he does so, then the plaintiff goes back to square one and must prove on the balance of probabilities that the defendant has been negligent. Support for this view can be found in *Colvilles Ltd v Devine* (1969).

- The other view is that it reverses the burden of proof

  The defendant must prove on the balance of probabilities, that he has not been negligent. Support for this view can be found in *Henderson v Jenkins* (1970) and *Ward v Tesco Stores* (1976). The Privy Council in *Ng Chun Pui v Lee Chuen Tat* (1988) stated that the burden of proof does not shift to the defendant but remains with the plaintiff throughout the case. It has also been argued that if *res ipsa loquitur* reverses the burden of proof then paradoxically a plaintiff who relies on the maxim will be in a better position than a plaintiff who establishes a *prima facie* case in some other way.

Causation

The plaintiff not only has to prove that the defendant owes him a duty of care and has breached his duty but also that the defendant caused the plaintiff's loss. This is not always as obvious as it sounds.

'But for' test

The defendant's breach of duty must as a matter of fact be a cause of the damage. As a preliminary test in deciding whether the defendant's breach has caused the plaintiff's damage, the courts have developed the 'but for' test. In other words, would the plaintiff not have suffered the damage 'but for' the event brought about by the defendant?

An example of the working of the test is contained in *Barnett v Chelsea and Kensington Hospital Management Committee* (1969). Three nightwatchmen called into a hospital at the end of a shift, complaining that they had been vomiting after drinking tea. The nurse on duty consulted a doctor by telephone and he said that the men should go home and consult their doctor in the morning. Later the same day the plaintiff's husband died of arsenical poisoning.

The doctor owed the plaintiff's husband a duty of care. In failing to examine the plaintiff's husband, the doctor had breached his duty of care but the hospital was held not to be liable as the breach had not caused the death. The plaintiff's husband would have died even if the doctor had examined him. Applying the 'but for' test, would the plaintiff not have suffered the damage 'but for' the event brought about by the defendant? The answer has to be no.

Further examples of the 'but for' test can be found in *Robinson v Post Office* (1974) where a doctor was held not to be liable for failing to administer a test dose of a drug where it would have failed to have revealed the allergy and in *McWilliams v Sir William Arrol and Co Ltd* (1962) where employers were found not to be liable for failing to provide a safety belt where it was proved that the employee would not have worn it even if it had been provided and *The Empire Jamaica* (1957) where liability was limited to 'actual fault' and the only fault that could be attributed to the owners was a failure to apply for a mate's certificate which would have been granted as a formality.

Nature of the 'but for' test

Students often fail to understand the true nature of the 'but for' test. It is vital to keep the following points in mind:

- it acts as a preliminary filter, ie it sifts irrelevant causes from relevant causes;
- it has no application where there are several successive causes of an accident.

Several successive causes

The 'but for' test will not be of much assistance where the plaintiff has been affected by two successive acts or events. In this type of situation, there has been a sequence of events and every act in the sequence is a relevant cause as far as the plaintiff's damage is concerned so the courts have to decide the operative cause.

The courts have not always been consistent in their approach. One method is to establish whether the later event has added to the plaintiff's damage, if not then the person who caused the original injury will be liable.

In *Performance Cars Ltd v Abraham* (1962), the plaintiff's Rolls Royce had been involved in an accident and the damage involved the cost of respraying the car. Two weeks later the defendant was involved in an accident with the plaintiff for which the defendant accepted responsibility. This time there was damage to the wing and bumper which necessitated a respray of the lower part of the car. The defendant was not liable as he had not contributed any more damage than had occurred after the first accident.

A similar sequence took place in *Baker v Willoughby* (1970). As a result of the defendant's negligence, the plaintiff suffered an injury to his left leg. Before the trial and while working at a new job the plaintiff was the victim of an armed robbery and suffered gunshot wounds to the same left leg which then had to be amputated. The defendants argued that their liability was extinguished by the second incident. In other words, they were only liable from the date of the accident to the date of the bank robbery. The House of Lords rejected this. They held that the plaintiff was being compensated for his loss of amenity, ie the loss of a good left leg, the difference between a damaged leg and a sound leg. The fact that the leg was further damaged at some later date did not alter the fact that he had already been deprived of the facility of a properly functioning left leg.

In both these cases, there have been two successive incidents and the second incident has not added to the plaintiff's loss so the perpetrator of the first incident has remained liable. This can be contrasted with *Jobling v Associated Dairies Ltd* (1982). The facts were that the defendants negligently caused an injury to the plaintiff's back. Three years later and before trial, the plaintiff was diagnosed as suffering from a condition called myelopathy which was unrelated to the accident. This time it was accepted, in contrast to the other cases, the second incident extinguished liability. The main differences between these cases have been identified as follows:

- in *Jobling*, the second incident occurred as a result of a natural condition, whereas in *Baker v Willoughby* there was an intervention by a third party;
- policy decisions on the part of the court (if the court had accepted that the second incident extinguished liability in *Baker* this would have left the defendant without compensation after the second incident).

Simultaneous events

The pragmatic approach of the courts was again evident in the case of *Fitzgerald v Lane* (1987). The facts were that the plaintiff crossed a pelican crossing when the red pedestrian light was showing, he was hit by the first defendant's car and thrown onto the car's windscreen, then onto the ground and while lying on the ground the second defendant ran over him. It was impossible to determine each defendant's contribution towards the injury. He could have suffered slight injuries from the first defendant and been badly injured by the second or *vice versa*. The court held that after taking into account the plaintiff's contributory negligence, both defendants were equally liable.

Multiple causes

So far we have looked at situations where there have been a sequence of events. Slightly different issues arise when there are several possible causes of an injury. Again, the courts approach has not always been consistent.

Where breach of duty materially increases the risk of injury, the defendant will be held liable

In *McGhee v National Coal Board* (1972), the defendants failed to supply adequate washing facilities. Although this could not be proved to have caused the defendant's dermatitis there was evidence to suggest that it had increased the risk of contracting the disease. This was sufficient to make the defendant liable.

The more recent trend is to state that for the defendant to be liable the defendant's cause must be the probable cause

In *Wilsher v Essex Area Health Authority* (1986), the plaintiff's injury could have been caused by one of six possible causes. One of these causes was the administration of an excess of oxygen in the first 30 hours of the baby's birth, which had been carried out by the doctor. It was held that the plaintiff had to prove that the excess of oxygen was the probable cause of the injury, not that it had increased the baby's risk of being born blind.

This approach was followed in *Hotson v East Berkshire Area Health Authority* (1987). The facts were that a boy fell out of a tree injuring his hip. He was rushed to hospital but the injury was not diagnosed for five days. The boy developed a hip condition. There was a 75% chance that the condition would have developed anyway and a 25% chance that the delay in diagnosis had caused the condition. The trial judge reduced damages by 75%. On appeal, it was held that this approach was incorrect. The defendants would not be liable unless their cause was the probable cause. As it was more likely that the condition would have developed anyway, then the most probable cause was that it had developed as a result of the fall. The defendants were not liable.

The approach in *Wilshier and Hotson* to decide causation questions has not been followed in other areas of negligence not involving personal injury. In a case the negligent misstatement case of *First Interstate Bank of California v Cohen Arnold & Co* (1995) damages were awarded on a basis that was proportionate to the likelihood of the event occurring. The defendants were a firm of accountants and, in a letter, grossly overestimated the worth of their client to the plaintiffs, a bank. As a result of the letter, the plaintiffs delayed enforcing their security. The property was sold for £1.4 million. If it had been sold when the bank first made inquiries as to the client's worth it would have been worth £3 million. There was a $66\frac{2}{3}$ chance that they would have sold when they first made inquiries, so damages were reduced to £2 million.

Intervening acts that break the chain of causation (*novus actus interveniens*)

Sometimes something can occur between the defendant's act and the plaintiff's injury, which breaks the chain of causation so the defendant can no longer be said to be liable to the plaintiff. This is a *novus actus interveniens*.

It was described by Lord Wright in *The Oropesa* (1943) as '... a new cause which disturbs the sequence of events, something which can be described as either unreasonable or extraneous or extrinsic'.

The facts of *The Oropesa* (1943) were that two ships collided. The captain of one ship put out to sea in heavy weather in a lifeboat to discuss the situation with the captain of the other ship and was drowned. It was argued that this constituted a *novus actus* but this was rejected as it was held that the decision to put out to sea was reasonable in the circumstances.

A rescuer's intervention will not be considered a *novus actus*, as long as the peril is active (*Haynes v Harwood* (1935)).

The courts have been quite lenient in what they consider to be a reasonable act. In *Philco Radio and Television Corporation of Great Britain Ltd v J Spurling and Others* (1949), it was held that the act of a typist in touching film scrap with a lighted cigarette with the intention of causing a 'small innocuous fire' but with the result that she caused a serious fire and explosion when the scrap had been wrongly delivered to the plaintiff's premises was not a *novus actus* as it was not an unreasonable act in the circumstances, even though it was unforeseeable.

For an intervening act to constitute a *novus actus*, it must be something in the order of an illegal act such as in *Knightley v John* (1982) where a police officer, contrary to police standing orders sent a police motor-cyclist the wrong way through a tunnel without first sealing the tunnel off. This constituted a *novus actus*.

However, not every illegal act constitutes a *novus actus*, as in *Rouse v Squires* (1973) where the court required a reckless, negligent act. The first defendant caused a motorway accident and a second driver who was driving too fast and failed to keep a proper look out collided with the stationary vehicles. The first driver was held partially to be responsible for the additional damage as the intervening conduct had not been so reckless as to constitute a *novus actus*. This element of recklessness was again required in *Wright v Lodge* (1993) where the first defendant negligently left her car on the carriageway in thick fog. The second defendant was deemed to be driving recklessly when he collided with the first defendant's car when driving at 60 mph before swerving across the carriageway and crashing into several cars. It was held that the second driver's recklessness broke the chain of causation and the first defendant could not be held liable for the damage suffered by the other drivers.

Knightley v Johns is hard to reconcile with *Rouse v Squires* and *Wright v Lodge* and the differences arise as a result of policy decisions on the part of the court. In the words of Stephenson LJ in *Knightley v Johns*, the court looks at 'common sense rather than logic on the facts and circumstances of each case'.

Acts of the plaintiff

The plaintiff's acts can constitute a *novus actus*, as in *McKew v Holland Hannen and Cubitts* (1969), the defendants had injured the plaintiff's left leg. One day, as the plaintiff was descending some stairs he felt that his leg was about to give way so he jumped down the remaining stairs, thereby injuring his right leg. The plaintiff's act constituted a *novus actus* as it had been an unreasonable act in the circumstances.

By contrast, in *Wieland v Cyril Lord Carpets* (1969) the plaintiff's neck had been injured by the defendants and as a consequence she was required to wear a surgical collar. She fell as she had been unable to use her bifocal spectacles with her usual skill and suffered further injuries. The additional injuries were held to be attributable to the defendants original negligence.

In *Kirkham v Chief Constable of Greater Manchester* (1990), it was held that the suicide of a prisoner in police custody was not a *novus actus*. The police were under a duty to guard the prisoner to prevent that type of incident occurring.

Remoteness of damage

Theoretically, the consequences of conduct are endless, so even where the defendant has breached a duty there must be some 'cut off' point beyond which the defendant will not be liable. If a defendant was responsible for his actions *ad infinitum* human activity would be unreasonably hampered.

Since 1850, there have been two competing views as to the test for remoteness of damage:

- consequences are too remote if a reasonable man would not have foreseen them (*The Wagon Mound* (1967));
- the defendant is liable for all the direct consequences of his act suffered by the plaintiff, whether a reasonable man would have foreseen them or not, no matter how unusual or unexpected (*Re Polemis and Furness, Withy & Co Ltd* (1921)).

The Wagon Mound lays down the rule that foreseeability of damage is the test not only for the imposition of a duty of care but also for remoteness of damage. Remember in this context we are looking at liability for the extent of damage, not whether a duty exists.

Manner of occurrence of damage need not be foreseeable

If the *type* of injury is foreseeable then the manner in which it occurs need not be foreseeable (*Hughes v Lord Advocate* (1963)) but note that this case was distinguished in *Doughty v Turner Manufacturing Co Ltd* (1964).

Type of injury must be foreseeable

In *Tremain v Pike* (1969), the plaintiff was a herdsman who was employed by the defendants and he contracted Weil's Disease, which is extremely rare and is caught by coming into contact with rats' urine. It was held that injury through food contamination was foreseeable, a 'rare disease' was a different type of injury and was not therefore foreseeable.

However, the House of Lords in *Page v Smith* (1995) awarded damages for psychiatric injury, even though only physical injury was foreseeable. It was held that in the case of primary victims of nervous shock there should be no distinction between physical and psychiatric injury.

The extent of the damage need not be foreseeable 'thin skull rule'

Provided the *type* of injury is foreseeable, the defendant will be liable for its full extent even if that is greater than could have been foreseen, due to some peculiar susceptibility, eg thin skull. This is a residuary hangover from the days of *Re Polemis*.

So, in *Bradford v Robinson Rentals* (1967), a lorry driver was subject to extreme cold and suffered frost bite as a result. The defendants were liable even though the injury was greater than could have been foreseen because the type of injury was foreseeable. This can be contrasted with *Tremain v Pike*, where the type of injury had not been foreseeable.

Impecuniosity of the plaintiff

There is a duty in tort to mitigate one's loss, ie not increase one's loss unnecessarily. Problems arise where the defendant is too impecunious to be able to afford to mitigate his loss. The courts have not always been consistent in their approach. In *Liesbosch Dredger v Edison SS* (1933), the plaintiff's had been put to much greater expense in fulfilling a contract because they were too poor to buy a substitute dredger for the one which had been damaged by the defendants. It was held that the plaintiff's impecuniosity had to be disregarded and they were unable to recover the additional expenses.

This can be contrasted with more recent cases such as *Dodd Properties Ltd v Canterbury City Council* (1980) and *Martindale v Duncan* where delays in repair caused by impecuniosity and the cost of substitute hire vehicles were allowed. It was said in *Mattocks v Mann* (1992) that *The Liesbosch* was constantly being changed in the light of changed circumstances and hire charges were again allowed.

2 Occupiers' liability

> **You should be familiar with the following areas:**
>
> - occupiers, visitors and trespassers
> - children, warnings and independent contractors
> - exclusion of duty
> - circumstances when a duty to a trespasser arises

Liability under the Occupiers' Liability Act 1957

Who is an 'occupier' for the purposes of the Act?

Common law rules apply
The Occupiers' Liability Act 1957 does not define the term occupier but stipulates that the rules of the common law shall apply (s 1(2)).

The test is one of control and not exclusive occupation
The basic test for an occupier is one of control over the premises. There can also be more than one occupier of premises, at any given time (*Wheat v E Lacon & Co Ltd* (1966)). The defendants owned a public house and the manager and his wife occupied the upper floor. The manager's wife was allowed to take paying guests and one of these guests had an accident on the staircase leading to the upper floor. It was held that the defendants were occupiers of the upper floor as they exercised residuary control.

It is not necessary to be present on the premises
In *Harris v Birkenhead Corporation* (1976), the local authority had issued a notice of compulsory purchase order and notice of entry but had not taken possession. They were held to be occupiers.

What is a 'visitor' for the purposes of the Act?

General category of visitor
The Occupiers' Liability Act 1957 replaces the old common law distinctions between 'invitees' and 'licensees' and replaces it with a general category of 'visitor'.

Express and implied permission

A visitor is someone who has express or implied permission to be on the land – either someone who has been expressly requested to enter onto premises or has permission to be there.

Knowledge of presence does not imply permission

The fact that the occupier knows of the plaintiff's presence or has failed to take steps to prevent entry does not mean that the occupier has given a licence (*Edwards v Railway Executive* (1952)).

Rules the same for children but may be a tacit licence

Knowledge that a track is constantly used by children together with a failure to take any steps to indicate that passage is not permitted does amount to a tacit licence (*Lowery v Walker* (1911)).

Entering premises to communicate with occupier does amount to tacit licence

A person entering with the purpose of communicating with the employer will have implied permission, eg, asking directions, the postman, roundsman, etc.

Entering premises to exercise a right conferred by law amounts to licence

Section 2(6) stipulates that anyone entering premises for any purpose in the exercise of a right conferred by law, are visitors, eg police with search warrants and officials empowered by statute to enter premises.

Exercising a public right of way does not constitute a licence

A person exercising a public right of way has no claim under the Occupiers' Liability Act 1957 because such a person was not an 'invitee' or 'licensee' at common law.

In *Greenhalgh v BRB* (1969), a railway bridge was built by the defendant's predecessor in title in 1873. In 1950, a housing estate was built either side of the railway bridge and the bridge was used to connect the two. The plaintiff was injured when he stepped in a pothole. It was held that the plaintiff was exercising a right of way and was not a 'visitor'.

This has recently been confirmed by the House of Lords in the Northern Irish case of *McGeown v Northern Ireland Housing Executive* (1994).

National Parks and Access to the Countryside Act 1949

Exercising rights under the National Parks and Access to the Countryside Act 1949, does not confer the status of a visitor.

The common duty of care

The Occupiers' Liability Act 1957 states that a common duty of care is owed by an occupier to all visitors except, insofar as he has extended, restricted, excluded or modified his duty.

The common duty of care is the duty to take such care as is reasonable to see that the visitor will be reasonably safe in using the premises for the purpose for which he is invited by the occupier to be there (s 2(2)).

Standard of care

The same standard of care as that which applies in ordinary negligence applies.

Guidelines

The Occupiers' Liability Act 1957 provides guidelines in the application of the common duty of care. Section 2(3) provides that the circumstances relevant for the purpose include the degree of care and want of care, which would ordinarily be looked for in such a visitor, so that (for example) in proper cases:

- an occupier must be prepared for children to be less careful than adults;
- an occupier must expect that a person, in exercise of his calling, will appreciate against any special risks ordinarily incident to his trade or calling.

Children

An occupier must be prepared for children to be less careful than adults. In *Moloney v Lambeth LBC* (1966), the occupier was liable when a four-year-old boy fell through a gap in railings protecting a stairwell, when an adult could not have fallen through the gap.

Allurements

An occupier must take precautions against children being attracted by allurements. In *Glasgow Corporation v Taylor* (1922), a seven-year-old boy ate poisonous berries on a visit to a botanical garden. It was held that the occupiers were liable as they knew that the berries were poisonous and they had made no attempt to fence the berries off.

Definition of allurements

Allurements were defined by Hamilton LJ in *Latham v R Johnson & Nephew Ltd* (1913) as something involving the idea of 'concealment and surprise, of an appearance of safety under circumstances cloaking a reality of danger'. So, in that case a child playing with a heap of stones had no remedy, as stones do not involve any element of allurement. In *Phipps v Rochester Corporation* (1955), a trench which was not concealed was held not to be an allurement and in *Simkiss v Rhondda BC* (1983) there was no concealed danger in sliding down a steep bluff on a blanket.

Skilled visitors

An occupier is entitled to expect that a person in the exercise of his calling will appreciate and guard against any special risks incidental to his trade.

In *Roles v Nathan* (1963), two chimney sweeps died from carbon monoxide poisoning while cleaning the flue of a boiler. They had been warned not to continue working while the boiler was alight. The occupier was held not to be liable as firstly, they had been warned of the danger and secondly, it was reasonable to expect a specialist to appreciate and guard against the dangers arising from the very defect that he had been called in to deal with.

The risk must be incidental to the trade or calling
In *Bird v King Line Ltd* (1970), it was held that the risks of working on a ship did not include falling on refuse which was carelessly left on the deck.

Occupier liability to skilled rescuers
In *Ogwo v Taylor* (1987), the occupier negligently started a fire and was liable to a fireman injured in the fire where the fire fighting operation has been carried out with due care.

Third parties

An occupier was held to be liable for the acts of third parties in *Cunningham v Reading FC* (1991). The defendants were liable when rioting fans broke lumps of concrete from a structure and used them as missiles, on the basis that a prudent occupier would have done more to minimise the risk.

Independent contractors

It will be a defence for the occupier to show that the defective state of the premises is caused by the faulty execution of work of construction, repair or maintenance by an independent contractor provided that:

- it was reasonable to entrust the work to an independent contractor;
- the occupier had taken reasonable care to see that the contractor was competent;
- the occupier had taken reasonable care to check that the work was reasonably done (s 2(4)(b)).

Reasonable to entrust work to a contractor

It depends on the circumstances and the nature of the work to be done as to whether it was reasonable to entrust the work to a contractor.

The more complex the work the more reasonable it will be to entrust it to a contractor. Thus, in *Haseldine v CA Daw & Son Ltd* (1941) an occupier was not liable for the negligence of an independent contractor in maintaining a lift in a block of flats. This can be contrasted with *Woodward v Mayor of Hastings* (1945) where the occupiers were liable for the negligence of a cleaner in leaving a step in an icy condition. Cleaning a step does not require any particular skill.

Discharge of the duty of care

Warning

Section 2(4)(a) provides that an occupier can discharge his duty to a visitor by giving a warning of the danger that in all the circumstances allows the visitor to be reasonably safe.

The test for determining whether a warning was adequate is a subjective one. A written warning will not be adequate in the case of someone who is blind or cannot read or speak English.

In *Staples v West Dorset District Council* (1995), it was held that an occupier had not been negligent when the council had failed to provide a warning and the danger was obvious. In such circumstances, a warning would not have told the visitor anything he did not already know and would not have affected his conduct.

Acceptance of the risk

Section 2(5) provides that an occupier does not have an obligation to a visitor in respect of risks willingly accepted by the visitor.

In *Simms v Leigh Rugby Football Club Ltd* (1969), the plaintiff had accepted the risks of playing on a rugby league ground which conformed to the by-laws of the Rugby League.

Knowledge of specific risk

In *White v Blackmore* (1972), it was held that it was insufficient to show that the plaintiff knew that jalopy car racing was dangerous, it was necessary to show that the plaintiff had consented to the specific risk that made that particular track dangerous.

Exclusion of liability

Section 2(1) provides that an occupier is able to, 'exclude, restrict or modify his duty'. In *Ashdown v Samuel Williams & Sons Ltd* (1957), the Court of Appeal accepted that a notice was sufficient to exclude liability. In *White v Blackmore*, notices put at the entrance to the field were sufficient to exclude liability.

Unfair Contract Terms Act

The Unfair Contract Terms Act 1977 has greatly restricted the occupiers ability to exclude his liability.

Premises used for business premises

As far as premises used for business purposes are concerned the occupier is unable to exclude liability for death and personal injury.

Exclusion of liability for other types of loss must satisfy the reasonableness test contained in s 7 of the Unfair Contract Terms Act 1977.

Premises used for private purposes

Occupiers of premises which are not in business use can only exclude liability if such exclusion is reasonable.

Occupiers' liability to trespassers

Common law rule

At common law, the original rule was that there was a mere duty not to deliberately or recklessly injure a trespasser (*Addie v Dumbreck* (1929)). There was a change of policy in the case of *BRB v Herrington* (1972) when it was held that an occupier was under a duty to act humanely towards trespassers. This was owed when a reasonable man knowing the physical facts which the occupier actually knew would appreciate that a trespasser's presence at the point and time of danger was so likely that in all the circumstances it would be inhumane not to give effective warning of the danger.

Occupiers' Liability Act 1984

The Occupiers' Liability Act 1984 replaces the common law to determine whether an occupier owes a duty to persons other than visitors.

Under s 1(3) of the 1984 Act, a duty is owed if:

- he is aware of the danger or has reasonable grounds to believe that it exists;
- he knows or has reasonable grounds to believe that the other person is in the vicinity of the danger concerned, or that he may come into the vicinity of danger (in either case whether the other has lawful authority for being in the vicinity or not); and
- the risk is one against which in all the circumstances of the case he may reasonably be expected to offer the other some protection.

Issues relating to the Occupiers' Liability Act 1984 arose in the case of *Revill v Newberry* (1995). The plaintiff was a trespasser attempting to break into a brick shed on an allotment belonging to the defendant. The defendant poked a shotgun through a small hole in the door and fired, injuring the plaintiff. The defendant had no means of knowing whether anyone was standing in front of the door. The plaintiff brought a claim in assault; under s 1 of the Occupiers' Liability Act 1984, and negligence. The claim for assault was dropped. Neill LJ argued that the Occupiers' Liability Act 1984 did not apply. The defendant was not being sued in his capacity as occupier with regard to the safety of the premises. The case had to be decided in accordance with the ordinary principles of negligence.

To whom does the Act apply?

The Occupiers' Liability Act 1984 applies to:

- trespassers;
- anyone exercising rights under the National Parks and Access to the Countryside Act 1949;
- anyone exercising a private right of way.

Discharge of the duty

Warning
Section 1(5) provides that the duty may be discharged by taking such steps as are reasonable in all the circumstances to warn of the danger concerned, or to discourage persons from incurring risk.

In *Cotton v Derbyshire Dales District Council* (1994), it was held that there was no duty to warn against dangers that are obvious.

Exclusion of liability
The Occupiers' Liability Act 1984 is silent on the question of whether the duty can be excluded with regard to trespassers. It has been argued that it is not possible to exclude a liability to a trespasser as it is a minimal duty.

3 Employers' liability

You should be familiar with the following areas:

Personal non-delegable duties

- provision of competent employees
- provision of safe plant and equipment
- provision of safe place of work
- provision of safe system of work

Vicarious liability

- tests for distinguishing between an employee and an independent contractor
- course of employment
- careless and deliberate acts
- masters' indemnity

Liability for independent contractors

- general rule that an employer is not vicariously liable for the wrongdoing of an independent contractor
- exceptions to the general rule

Personal non-delegable duties

Historical background

Doctrine of common employment

The case of *Priestly v Fowler* (1837) laid down the doctrine of common employment. Under this doctrine an employer was not liable to an employee for a tort committed by a fellow employee. This was based on the judicial fiction that an employee impliedly agreed to accept the risks incidental to his employment, including the risk of negligence of his fellow employees.

The courts had been heavily influenced by policy considerations that if they permitted compensation for industrial accidents this would place a heavy burden on employers.

Contributory negligence
Although under the doctrine the employee was said to take on the risk of negligence by fellow employees, he did not take on the risk of his employer being negligent and could sue his employer but only in the absence of contributory negligence on the employee's part.

Volenti non fit injuria
If an employee knew of the risk he would be considered *volenti non fit injuria* and again his claim would be defeated.

'Unholy trinity'
The combination of the doctrine of common employment, contributory negligence and *volenti non fit injuria* became known as an 'unholy trinity' and prevented virtually all actions by employees.

Mitigating the harshness of common employment
Various devices were developed to mitigate the harshness of the doctrine of common employment. The latter half of the 19th century saw a swing in favour of the workman.

Breach of statutory duty
The case of *Groves v Lord Wimborne* (1898) held that an employer was liable to a workman for an injury caused by a breach of statutory duty. If a duty was placed on an employer by statute, the employer did not escape liability if he delegated performance to another.

Volenti non fit injuria
It was held in *Smith v Baker and Sons* (1891) that the *volenti* defence would rarely apply to employees, as they said that there had to be free consent when the employee ran the risk.

No fault compensation
In 1897 an injured workman could receive compensation independently of the law when a no fault compensation scheme for work accidents was introduced by the Workman's Compensation Act 1897. In 1948, the National Insurance (Industrial Injuries) Act 1946 came into force whereby benefits became payable to victims of industrial diseases and virtually everyone employed under a contract of service or apprenticeship became entitled to benefits under the scheme. The National Insurance (Industrial Injuries) Act 1946 has now been replaced by the Social Security Act 1975.

Today, only 12.5% of those injured at work receive compensation through the tort system.

Development of personal non-delegable duties

Although the principle was developed that an employer was liable to an employee for his own negligence, this was increasingly of less use to employees as the 19th century progressed since more and more people were being employed by companies. To succeed under this principle it was necessary for there to be some element of 'personal fault' on the part of the employer. It was impossible for there to be some personal fault on the part of the employer where the employer was not a human being but a limited company with independent legal personality.

Such an employer could only act through his servants and if they were negligent the employer was not liable under the doctrine of common employment.

Non-delegable personal duties were created and owed by the employer to the employee. The employer remained responsible for the performance of these duties even though performance may have been delegated to an employee.

Duty to provide proper appliances

In the case of *Smith v Baker and Sons*, it was held that an employer owed a duty to an employee to provide proper appliances, when Lord Herschell said:

> It is quite clear that the contract between employer and employed involves on the part of the former the duty to take reasonable care to provide proper appliances, and to maintain them in a proper condition and so to carry on the operations as not to subject those employed by him to unnecessary risk.

Development of a threefold duty

In the later case of *Wilsons and Clyde Coal Co v English* (1938). the duty was said to be threefold, when Lord Wright said the duty was, 'the provision of a competent staff of men, adequate material, and a proper system and effective supervision'. To add to these three duties it has also become clear from the cases that there is also a duty to provide safe access to premises.

Abolition of the doctrine of common employment

The doctrine of common employment was abolished by s 1 of the Law Reform (Personal Injuries) Act 1948. An employer can now be vicariously liable to an employee for the negligence of a fellow employee.

Continuing importance of the primary duties

Despite the abolition of the doctrine of common employment, the primary duties still have an importance in two situations:

- An employer is only vicariously liable for torts committed 'in the course of employment', of an employee. An employer may not be vicariously liable for an employee's tort, since it was not committed in the course of employment but he could still have breached a primary duty.
- Vicarious liability does not extend to an independent contractor but an employer may still be liable to an employee where he has entrusted work to an independent contractor.

Employer's personal duties

Duty to provide competent staff

At common law, an employer owes a duty to an employee to select competent fellow employees.

The duty has lost some of its importance since the abolition of the doctrine of common employment but still retains its importance in one area. The courts are reluctant to make employers vicariously liable for the violent acts of an employee which are regarded as being outside the course of employment. The same can be argued of acts of horseplay. Both these examples may constitute breach of the primary duty to provide competent staff.

An employer will have breached his primary duty where an employee is injured by the foreseeable horseplay of a fellow employee. In *Hudson v Ridge Manufacturing Co Ltd* (1957), an employer breached his primary duty where an employee was injured by a fellow employee, who was a notorious prankster. The employer should have put an end to the pranks.

An employer is not liable where the horseplay is unforeseeable. In *Smith v Crossley Bros* (1951), the plaintiff suffered severe internal injuries when a fellow apprentice approached him from behind and placed a compressed air pipe close to his rectum and signalled to another employee to switch on the compressed air. In this case, it was held that the employer could not have foreseen that the apprentice would have done such a thing.

Proper plant and equipment

It was laid down by Lord Hershell in *Smith v Baker and Sons* (1891) that an employer has a 'duty of taking reasonable care to provide proper appliances, and to maintain them in a proper condition'.

At common law, there was no employer's liability for defects in manufacture. An employer was not liable for a defect in the manufacture of a tool, when this defect could not have been discovered on a reasonable inspection in *Davie v New Merton Board Mills Ltd* (1959).

Employer's Liability (Defective Equipment) Act 1969

To circumvent the problem caused by the common law, the Employers' Liability (Defective Equipment) Act 1969 was passed and an employer is now liable for an injury to an employee suffered in the course of employment as a result of a defect in a tool supplied by an employer and the defect is attributable to the fault of a third party, whether identifiable or not.

The Act relieves the employee of the need to identify and sue the manufacturer, if the equipment is provided by the employer.

Proper use

It was held in *Parkinson v Lyle Shipping Co* (1964) that the employer will not be liable where the employee has made improper use of the equipment.

Negligently choosing the wrong tool

In *Leach v British Oxygen Co* (1965), the employer was not liable where the employee foolishly chose the wrong tool, assuming that the employee had been given adequate instruction in the use of the equipment.

Meaning of equipment

The term 'equipment' was considered in *Coltman v Bibby Tankers Ltd* (1988). The question raised by the case was whether a ship came within the meaning of 'equipment' for the purposes of the Employers' Liability (Defective Equipment) Act 1969. The Court of Appeal held that it was not equipment because equipment was ancillary to something else and did not encompass the workplace. The House of Lords rejected this test and held that equipment did not have to be part of a larger whole and that there was no reason to exclude ships from the Act.

The House of Lords in *Knowles v Liverpool City Council* (1993) held that the Employers' Liability (Defective Equipment) Act 1969 was to be widely construed and embraced every article provided by the employer for the purpose of the business. So a flagstone came within the meaning of the Act.

Safe place of work

This duty was not expressly mentioned by Lord Wright in *Wilsons and Clyde Coal Co v English* (1938). However, it is clear that the employer's duty extends to providing a safe place of work and that this is a higher duty than that laid down in the Occupier's Liability Act 1957.

Means of access
In *Ashdown v Samuel Williams and Son Ltd* (1957), it was held that the duty extended to providing a safe means of access to the place of work.

Duty is discharged with reasonable care
The employer in *Latimer v AEC Ltd* (1953) was held to have taken reasonable care when he sprinkled a slippery factory floor with sawdust.

Duty not discharged by a warning
An employer did not discharge his duty by giving a warning in *London Graving Dock Co v Horton* (1951). Nor can an employer argue that the plaintiff was familiar with the danger and made no complaint (*McCafferty v Metropolitan Police District Receiver* (1977)).

Temporary danger
It was said in relation to temporary danger in *O'Reilly v National Rail and Tramways Appliances Ltd* (1966) that in cases of temporary danger the reasonableness of the employer's conduct would depend on the degree of the risk and the employer's knowledge of the risk.

Third party premises
At one time, the employer was thought not to be liable where the employee was working on premises that belonged to a third party.

It was held in *Wilson v Tyneside Window Cleaning Co* (1958) that an employer could be liable where the employee was working on third party premises. The steps required to discharge that duty will depend on the circumstances:

> The master's own premises are under his control: if they are dangerously in need of repair he can and must rectify the fault at once. But if a master sends his plumber to mend a leak in a private house, no one could hold him negligent for not visiting the house himself to see if the carpet in the hall creates a trap. Between these two extremes are countless possible examples in which the court must decide the question of fact: Did the master take reasonable care?

The duty does not extend to injuries caused by a defective floor in premises occupied by another employer when the employee was working in Saudi Arabia (*Square D Ltd v Cook* (1992)). There was no reason for the employer to suppose that the employer in Saudi Arabia was anything other than competent. This seems to create an exception to the rule that the duties are non-delegable.

Safe system of work

Whether an operation needs a safe system of work or can be left to a particular employee is a question of fact.

Regular or routine work

It was held in *Speed v Thomas Swift and Co* (1943) that the duty will normally apply in respect of a system of working which is regular or routine.

Single tasks

The duty can apply to a single task, where it is complicated or highly dangerous or prolonged or involves a number of men performing a number of different functions (*Winter v Cardiff RDC* (1950)).

Employer must check that the system is complied with

In *General Cleaning Contractors v Christmas* (1953), it was held that the employer must check that the system is being complied with. Although Lord Denning said that this was a proposition of good sense, so, for example, if a workman is provided with protective clothing it is not necessary to check that he actually wears it. In the words of Viscount Simmonds: 'I deprecate any tendency to treat the relation of employer and skilled workman as equivalent to that of nurse and imbecile child.'

Psychiatric damage

It was held in *Walker v Northumberland County Council* (1994) that the duty to provide a safe system of work includes a duty to take care of the employee's psychiatric, as well as physical, well being. The plaintiff had a nervous breakdown when trying to cope with an increased workload. On his return to work, he advised his superior that assistance would be required. An assistant was provided but helped intermittently and after a period of one month was unable to assist at all. The plaintiff then suffered a second breakdown and was unable to return to work. The defendant argued that it was not foreseeable that the plaintiff's work would impose such stress as to cause mental illness. It was held that the defendant was liable for the second breakdown, as it was a foreseeable consequence of the failure to relieve the pressure of work.

An employer was also liable for negligently causing psychiatric injury to employees in *Frost v Chief Constable of South Yorkshire* (1996).

Secondary employer

An employer who lends an employee to another employer was entitled to a complete indemnity against that employer for failure to provide suitable equipment and a safe system of work for the employee (*Needhams v Sandells Maintenance Ltd* (1995)). Although the employee can sue either employer, the first employer has a right of indemnity from the second.

Window cleaning
It was held in *King v Smith* (1994) that a window cleaner's customer should be made responsible for ensuring that where windows are capable of being cleaned from the inside, that they should be in proper working order to allow that to be done. The employee should also have been instructed by his employer not to clean windows from the outside where they were capable of being cleaned from the inside, if they had been in proper working order.

Battle conditions
In *Mulcahy v Ministry of Defence* (1996) a gun commander, during the Gulf War, negligently ordered the firing of a gun, thereby injuring the plaintiff. It was held that there was no duty in battle conditions to maintain a safe system of work.

Economic benefit of employees
The personal duties provide protection for the physical well being of employees. It is clear from *Reid v Rush and Tomkins Group plc* (1989) that the economic welfare of employees is not so well protected. The plaintiff was employed by the defendants and was sent to work in Ethiopia where he suffered severe injuries in a road accident caused by the negligence of another driver. After he failed to receive compensation he argued that the defendants should have advised him to take out insurance. It was held that no duty existed to protect an employee against economic loss, although it may arise out of a particular set of facts, eg a *Hedley Byrne* relationship.

Breach of statutory duty

Breach of statutory duty is the second head of liability an employer may have at common law. It is an entirely separate tort from negligence (considered more fully in the next chapter) and has been consistently allowed in the field of industrial safety, in marked contrast to other areas.

Its use began as a way of mitigating the harshness of the rule of common employment. Whereas the primary duties exist generally, wherever the employer – employee relationship exists, there is no such generalisation with statutory duties and the duty depends on the statute.

Health and Safety at Work Act 1974

The Health and Safety at Work Act 1974 consolidated many existing health and safety statutes. The Act imposes a number of general duties on employers. General duties have been added to by the Health and Safety at Work Regulations 1992. Breach of these duties gives rise to a penal sanction and a civil right of action is expressly excluded.

The 1974 Act gives the Secretary of State the power to bring forward regulations to cover the specific areas which are dealt with by existing legislation. Breach of the specific duties will give rise to a right to a civil action for breach of statutory duty, unless the regulation expressly states otherwise. In January 1993, six regulations became effective in the UK as a result of EC directives and have become known as the 'six pack'. These add to the list of specific statutory duties in respect of specific dangers.

Defective equipment

Employers are strictly liable for injuries to employees caused by defective equipment under the Employers' Liability (Defective Equipment) Act 1969.

Factories Act 1961

This consolidates earlier Factories Acts. Sections 12–16 cover the fencing of machinery and the rule is that 'every dangerous part' must be fenced. It was held in *Davies v Thomas Owen and Co* (1919) that this is an absolute duty.

Vicarious liability

Vicarious liability exists when A is liable to C for damages caused by B. Thus it is liability for actions of another. The most important instance of vicarious liability is that of employer and employee.

Who is an employee?

The courts have used various criteria in deciding the difficult question of whether a tortfeasor is an employee for the purposes of vicarious liability. If the employee fails to come within the criteria then the tortfeasor will not be an employee but an independent contractor for whom with exceptions, the employer is not vicariously liable.

- Employee – contract for service.
- Independent contractor – contract for services.
- Certain criteria are to be taken into account in cases where uncertainty exists.

Intention of the parties

This is relevant but not conclusive, even if the contract expressly states that the worker is an independent contractor.

In *Ferguson v Dawson Partners (Contractors) Ltd* (1976), the contract of a building worker stated that a worker was 'labour only sub-contractor' but was nevertheless held to be an employee because he was treated as an employee for all other purposes.

'The control test'

The traditional test is in terms of control, ie *degree* of control. Where substantial control of the working conditions of the worker are being exercised the more likely it is that the worker is an employee. However, this will not apply to the same extent with skilled workers. For example, a hospital does not control a surgeon in the performance of an operation.

Integration within the business

The extent to which a worker is 'integral' to the business or merely 'accessory' to it may be the deciding factor, *per* Lord Denning in *Stevenson Jordan & Harrison Ltd v MacDonald & Evans* (1952). If a worker is integral then he will be an employee; if the worker is an accessory then he is an independent contractor.

Allocation of financial risks

As a general rule, employees work for a wage which is calculated by reference to the time worked. Employees are not required to run the risk of financial loss and they do not share in the profits.

In *Ready Mixed Concrete (South East) Ltd v Minister of Pensions and National Insurance* (1968), a company organised its deliveries through owner drivers. The drivers were required to buy their vehicles on HP from an associated finance company, vehicles had to be painted in the company colours, the 'owner-driver' could not alter, charge or sell the vehicle without the company's permission and the company had an option to purchase the vehicle, it could not be used for private purposes and the 'owner-driver' had to comply with the rules and regulations of the company.

It was held that despite the extensive control exercised over the 'owner-drivers' the terms were more consistent with a contract of carriage rather than a contract of service. Particular emphasis was placed on the fact that the 'owner-driver' had to make the vehicle available throughout the contract period at his own expense and the chance of profit or risk of loss was the driver's.

Changing nature of employment

The changing nature of employment is making it increasingly difficult to distinguish between an employee and someone who is self-employed. In *Lane v Shire Roofing Company (Oxford) Ltd* (1995), the plaintiff had been self-employed but his business encountered difficulties. He agreed to work for the defendants under a large sub-contract they had obtained. He was injured when he fell off a ladder.

There were indications pointing both ways. First, the defendant was a new company and did not wish to take on employees. Secondly, the plaintiff was in business on his own account and was capable of working without supervision. Thirdly, there was no guarantee of more work and no provision for notice or dismissal.

Henry LJ paid regard to the changing nature of the employment market and the growth in flexible working. He asked the question: whose business is it? On this basis he held that it was the defendant's and that the plaintiff was an employee.

However, it is hard to see any new general principles emerging. In *McMeechen v Secretary of State for Employment* (1995), the plaintiff worked for an employment agency. He was described as self-employed. On the other hand, he was paid weekly and the terms of his contract seemed to accord with that of an employee. He was held to be self-employed.

Employees on loan

A problem arises when an employee is lent by one employer to another. Which one is liable for the acts of the employee?

In *Mersey Docks and Harbour Board v Coggins & Griffith* (1946), a crane driver was lent by a harbour authority to a firm of stevedores. The conditions of hire stated that the crane driver was to be considered a servant of the stevedores but they had no power to tell the driver how to work his crane. It was held that the harbour authority was liable for the crane driver's negligence.

Course of employment

The tort must be committed in the course of the employee's employment. This is a question of fact. One test is that an act is within the course of employment if it is either:

- a wrongful act authorised by the employer; or
- a wrongful and unauthorised mode of doing some authorised act.

Carelessness of employee

If the employer is doing the job he is authorised to do but contrary to the manner in which he has been instructed to do it, then the employer will be vicariously liable. In *Whatman v Pearson* (1868), the employer instructed his employees that they were not to go home or leave their horses during their dinner break. An employee went home and in his absence his horse damaged the plaintiff's property.

In *Storey v Ashton* (1869), an employer was not liable for a negligently caused road accident because at the time of the accident his employee had taken a detour to transact some private business.

Similarly, in *Crook v Derbyshire Stone Ltd* (1956) an employer whose employee negligently caused an accident in his meal break was not liable for the acts of the employee.

Violence by employee

An employer will not be liable for the violent acts of an employee as they are outside the course of employment. In *Warren v Henlys Ltd* (1948), a pump attendant hit a customer whom he wrongly suspected of not paying. It was held to be an act of personal vengeance and therefore outside the course of employment.

This can be contrasted with the case of *Daniels v Whetstone Entertainments* (1962) where a bouncer who was authorised to use such force as was necessary inside a night-club, hit someone during the course of a fracas inside the night-club and then followed the person outside and hit them again. It was held that the second act was outside the course of employment.

An employee is also entitled to use reasonable force in defence of person or property. In *Poland v Parr & Sons* (1927), an off duty employee saw some boys apparently stealing from one of his employer's wagons. He stuck one of the boys who fell and was run over. It was held that an employee has an implied authority to act for the protection of his employer's property.

Express prohibition

Here it is necessary to distinguish between the employee doing his job in a manner in which he has been instructed not to do it, for which the employer will be vicariously liable and performing a task which the employee has been told is outside the scope of his job.

So, the employer was liable in *Limpus v London General Omnibus Co* (1862) when the employee raced his vehicle and obstructed another vehicle, when the employee had been instructed not to do this, as it was an unauthorised mode of performing an authorised act.

Contrast that case with *Iqbal v LTE* (1973) where a bus conductor had been told on many occasions not to move buses and the employer was consequently not liable when the conductor injured someone while moving a bus in the depot. Driving was outside the scope of the conductor's employment.

The House of Lords held in *Racz v Home Office* (1993) that the Home Office would be vicariously liable for acts of prison officers that amounted to misfeasance in public office unless the acts were so unconnected with their authorised duties as to be independent of and outside them, which is a question of fact and degree.

Theft and fraud

Employers are liable for acts of theft and fraud committed by employees. In *Morris v CW Martin & Sons Ltd* (1966), a firm of dry cleaners were liable for the theft of a coat by an employee.

Similarly, in *Lloyd v Grace Smith & Co* (1912) a firm of solicitors were liable for the fraud of a managing clerk who fraudulently conveyed properties belonging to a client to himself.

Master's indemnity

There is an implied term in an employee's contract of employment that the employee will exercise reasonable care when performing his duties. Where an employee's negligence leads to an employer's vicarious liability then at common law the employer is entitled to be indemnified for the loss attributable to the employee's breach of contract.

In *Lister v Romford Ice & Coal Storage Co Ltd* (1957), the defendant was an employee of the plaintiff and had injured another employee, the defendant's father. The defendant's father obtained damages against the plaintiff who then sought to be indemnified by the defendant. It was held that the plaintiff was entitled to this indemnity.

Liability for independent contractors

General rule

The general rule is that an employer is not liable for the torts of an independent contractor. The rationale for this rule is that an employer does not exercise control over an independent contractor. There are a number of important exceptions to this rule.

Exceptions to the general rule

Authorised or ratified tort
Ellis v Sheffield Gas Consumers (1853) is authority for the proposition that the employer will be a joint tortfeasor where he has authorised or ratified the tort.

Negligence in choosing the contractor
Pinn v Rew (1916) is authority for the proposition that an employer will be liable if he negligently chooses an independent contractor, fails to instruct him properly or fails to check the work where he is competent to do so.

Non-delegable duties imposed by common law

Rule in Rylands v Fletcher
Rylands v Fletcher is a rule of strict liability and the employer will be liable for the acts of an independent contractor.

Extra hazardous operations
Where the independent contractor is involved in an extra hazardous activity, which has been defined as something which involves the risk of special danger to others then the employer will be liable (*Honeywill and Stein Ltd v Larkin Bros Ltd* (1934)).

Liability for fire
In *Balfour v Barty-King* (1957), the defendant negligently thawed pipes with a blow lamp, thus negligently setting fire to the plaintiff's property. The defendant was held liable for the contractor's negligence.

Operations which are on or contiguous to the highway
In *Tarry v Ashton* (1876), the defendant's lamp which projected over the highway fell and injured the plaintiff. The fact that the defendant had delegated repair of the lamp to an independent contractor was no defence.

Common law duties owed by an employer to an employee
These duties are personal and cannot be delegated.

Non-delegable duties imposed by statute
Strict and absolute duties imposed under statute are non-delegable, eg Factories Act 1961.

Bailee for reward

A bailee for reward who entrusts goods to an independent contractor, remains liable for any loss or damage to the goods, in the absence of a contractual provision to the contrary (*Morris v CW Martin and Sons Ltd* (1966)).

No liability for collateral negligence

For the employer to be liable, the tortiously performed act of the independent contractor must be one he was employed to do and not an act unconnected with what he was employed to do (*Padbury v Holliday and Greenwood Ltd* (1912)).

4 Breach of statutory duty

You should be familiar with the following areas:

- Lord Denning's test in *Ex parte Island Records*
- reaffirmation of the traditional test in *Lonrho v Shell Petroleum Co Ltd (No 2)*;
- exceptions where civil right of action will be allowed, rule is for the benefit of a class where an individual has suffered particular damage
- the elements of breach of statutory duty
- defences of voluntary assumption of the risk; contributory negligence and act of a third party
- proposals for reform

Original principle

The early cases on breach of statutory duty rested on a broad principle that whenever a violation of a statute caused damage to an individual's interests a right of action in tort arose.

Recent attempts to resurrect broad principle

Lord Denning MR attempted to resurrect the broad principle in *Ex Parte Island Records* (1978) when he said that whenever a private right had been interfered with, causing an individual special damage over and above that suffered by the rest of the public, then he would have a civil right of action.

If the 'broad Denning principle' had been accepted then it would have transformed actions for breach of statutory duty and allowed greater protection of economic and business interests by the law of tort.

Reaffirmation of the narrower principle

The House of Lords rejected the broad principle in the case of *Lonrho v Shell Petroleum Co Ltd (No 2)* (1981) and reasserted the general rule that 'where an act creates an obligation and enforces performance in a specified manner ... that performance cannot be enforced in any other manner'. There are two classes of exception to the general rule. First, where it can be seen that the obligation has been imposed for the benefit of a class of people, such as employees. Secondly, where an individual suffers particular damage over and above the rest of the public when a public right has been infringed.

So in answer to the question, 'Does the statute give rise to civil liability?' the possibilities are as follows:

- the statute in question may state that civil liability will or will not arise from a breach of the Act, if so, then it is clear whether civil liability arises; or
- the Act is silent on the question of civil liability and it will then be a question of construction of the statute to determine if civil liability exists. Where there is a remedy laid down in the statute there will be a presumption that no civil liability exists unless the case comes within the two exceptions of the obligation being for the benefit of a class or an individual who has suffered particular damage over and above that suffered by the rest of the public.

Statutory remedy

As a general rule if the Act provides a remedy then this is the only remedy permitted. This tends to exclude many statutes which are criminal in nature and provide for some type of penalty.

In *Lonrho Ltd v Shell Petroleum Co Ltd* (1981), the House of Lords approved the general rule laid down by Lord Tenterden CJ in *Doe d Bishop of Rochester v Bridges* (1831), namely that 'where an act creates an obligation, and enforces the performance in a specified manner ... that performance cannot be specified in any other manner'.

An illustration of the working of this rule can be seen in *Atkinson v Newcastle Waterworks Co* (1877) when a penalty of £10 existed for a breach of the Waterworks Clauses Act 1847 for failure to maintain sufficient water pressure which precluded the plaintiff from bringing an action for breach of statutory duty, when his premises burnt down because there was no water. The fine provided the method of enforcement of the duty.

A rather different line was taken in *Groves v Lord Wimborne* (1898) where an employee was able to bring a civil action even though there was a penalty of up to £100 for breach of the duty. The court was influenced by the fact that there was no requirement to apply the penalty in favour of the defendant and the set limit might be insufficient to compensate the plaintiff fully. The employer-employee relationship has been one area where the courts have been willing to allow actions for breach of statutory duty, principally because health and safety legislation is considered to be for the benefit of a class, ie employees.

Rights of appeal from a decision through administrative channels with an ultimate right of judicial review constitutes a remedy (*E v Dorset County Council; Christmas v Hampshire County Council; Keating v Bromley London Borough Council* (1994)). The statutory code providing for the identification, assessment and assistance for children with special education needs under the Education Acts 1944 and 1981 and regulations made thereunder did not give rise to a right of action for breach of statutory duty since there was an appeal procedure open to parents who wished to challenge decisions. If parents were not satisfied with the appeals procedure they could apply for judicial review.

Common law remedy

Where a common law remedy is available then it is felt that the courts should not admit civil liability for breach of statutory duty. Authority for this can be found in *Phillips v Britannia Hygienic Laundry Co Ltd* (1923).

However, an action for breach of statutory duty will be allowed where it supplements the common law. In *Monk v Warbey* (1935), the defendant allowed an uninsured driver to drive his car contrary to s 35 of the Road Traffic Act 1930. The driver negligently injured the plaintiff but the judgment remained unsatisfied. The plaintiff was allowed to succeed against the defendant.

Two further aspects of the incidence of an action for breach of statutory duty were raised by way of exceptions to the general rule for breach of statutory duty by Lord Diplock in the *Lonrho Ltd* case:

- where the obligation/prohibition was imposed for the benefit or protection of a class of individuals; and
- where the statute creates a public right and an individual member of the public suffers 'particular damage'.

Benefit of a class

Where the statute was passed for the benefit of an ascertainable class of individuals the presumption is that an action will lie, *per* Lord Diplock in *Lonrho Ltd.*

The purpose of the Dramatic and Musical Performers' Protection Act 1958 in *Rickless v United Artists Corpn* (1988) was found to be the protection of performers' rights and financial interests. The plaintiffs could therefore bring an action for the unauthorised use of clips from old Peter Sellers' films.

Recent cases have shown that there must be an intention on the part of the legislature to confer on the class a right for damages for the breach. Lord Bridge in *Pickering v Liverpool Daily Post and Echo Newspapers plc* (1991) said:

> ... it must ... appear upon the true construction of the legislation in question that the intention was to confer on members of the protected class a cause of action sounding in damages occasioned by the breach.

This followed similar *dicta* by Lord Bridge in *Calveley v Chief Constable of the Merseyside Police* (1989).

In *Hague v Deputy Governor of Parkhurst Prison* and *Weldon v Home Office* (1991), prisoners who had suffered injury as a result of breaches of the Prison Rules could not bring an action for breach of statutory duty. The aim of the Prison Act 1952 (under which the regulations had been made) was to deal with the management and control of prisons and prisoners. The aims were wider than simply the protection of prisoners. Lord Jauncey compared the Prison Act to the Factories Acts where the main aim had been the protection of the health and safety of employees and the duty could therefore be said to be for the benefit of a class.

The House of Lords again stated the rules in *X v Bedfordshire County Council*; *M v Newham LBC* and *Keating v Bromley LBC* (1995). Local authorities had breached their duties to protect children under the Children and Young Persons Act 1969, the Child Care Act 1980, the Children Act 1989 and the Education Acts 1944 and 1981. Such duties are designed to protect children but a right of action for breach of statutory duty did not arise, as there was no parliamentary intention to confer a private right of action on that class.

The principles laid down in *Hague* and *X v Bedfordshire County Council* were followed in *Olotu v Home Office* (1996). The plaintiff had been committed for trial and was held in custody for 112 days. At the expiry of 112 days, the Crown Prosecution Service failed to bring her before the Crown Court to have the period extended and she spent 81 days in prison in excess of the time limit. It was said that the object of the Prosecution of Offences Act 1985 and the Prosecution of Offences (Custody Time Limits) Regulations 1987 was to expedite the prosecution of criminal offences and to ensure, if expedition was lacking, that defendants did not languish in prison for excessive periods awaiting trial. There was, however, nothing to suggest that Parliament intended to create new private law rights of action.

Public right where particular damage suffered

Lord Diplock's second exception was where the statute creates a public right and an individual member of the public suffers 'particular damage'. It is not exactly clear how this category is to be identified.

Elements of the tort

Duty imposes an obligation on the defendant

The statute imposes an obligation on the defendant. This includes obligations imposed under the EC Treaty. In *Garden Cottage Foods Ltd v Milk Marketing Board* (1984), a breach of Article 86 which prohibits abuse of a dominant position by a company gave rise to a right for breach of statutory duty.

Duty must be owed to the plaintiff

In *Hartley v Mayoh* (1954), a fire broke out in the factory premises of the first defendants. On arrival at the scene, one of the officers of the fire brigade went to locate the main electrical switches in order to cut off the electric supply to the premises. He was directed to the main switchboard by the factory manager and switched off two master switches but was not directed to two smaller switches.

The effect was that the electrical current was not switched off to the entire premises. One of the fire officers was electrocuted and died. His widow sued for negligence and for breach of statutory duty.

The statutory duty was expressed to be owed to 'persons employed'. As the fireman was not an employee, he was not a person for whose benefit the duty had been made and an action did not lie for breach of statutory duty.

Injury should be of a kind the statute is intended to prevent

The leading case is *Gorris v Scott* (1874). A statutory order required parts of a ship occupied by animals to be divided into pens of a specified size. The defendant violated this order and the plaintiff's sheep were washed overboard. The order was intended to prevent the spread of disease, not to prevent animals from being drowned, so an action for breach of statutory duty failed.

The harm suffered by the plaintiff must be within the general class of risks at which the statute is directed. For example, the duty imposed on highway authorities to repair roads is to protect road users from injury. Consequently, there cannot be a right of action where the poor state of repair leads to loss of profits for a local trader (*Wentworth v Wiltshire County Council* (1993)).

There must be a breach of statute

It was held in *Chipcase v British Titan Products* (1956) that a statutory duty which applied to platforms of more than 6 ft 6 in from the ground does not apply to a platform that is only 6 ft from the ground. No breach, no action.

The breach must have caused the damage

It is for the plaintiff to show that the breach caused the damage. In *Ginty v Belmont Building Supplies* (1959), the plaintiff was employed by the first defendant to replace the asbestos sheeting on the second defendant's roof. The Building (Safety, Health and Welfare) Regulations 1948 required boards not only to be provided but to be (vicariously) used. The plaintiff was told where he could obtain duckboards. When he was seen not to be using them they were put out for his use. The plaintiff fell and sustained injury.

It was held that the plaintiff could not recover damages as the accident had been his own fault.

Defences

Relationship between criminal and tortious liability

Breaches of particular statutory duties may give rise both to criminal and tortious proceedings. It must not, however, be assumed that the defences in each case are identical.

Assumption of risk

It was held in *Wheeler v New Merton Board Mills Ltd* (1933) that *volenti non fit injuria* is not a defence to an action brought by an employee for breach of a statutory duty by an employer. *Wheeler* was approved by the House of Lords in *Imperial Chemical Industries Ltd v Shatwell* (1965) but it added that the defence of *volenti* should be available where the employer had not himself or vicariously breached the statutory duty.

Contributory negligence

At common law, contributory negligence was a defence. Apportionment of damages is now available under the Law Reform (Contributory Negligence) Act 1945.

Particular problems arise in the employer-employee relationship. In carrying out duties under health and safety legislation employers are supposed to take into account that people through constant repetition become careless for their own safety.

It was held in *Boyle v Kodak Ltd* (1969) that where the employer had delegated performance of the duty and the employer can prove that the only reason why the Act has not been complied with is because the plaintiff's act or default, then that is a good defence, even where the employer is under strict liability.

Act of third party

This is not a defence where the statute imposes strict liability on the defendant.

Proposals for reform

In 1969 the Law Commission in The Interpretation of Statutes recommended a single reform. Actions for breach of statutory duty would have to be specifically excluded in the Act, even where there is a remedy for the Act's enforcement.

5 Intentional interference with the person

> **You should be familiar with the following areas:**
> - the elements of trespass
> - the elements of assault, battery and false imprisonment
> - the defences to trespass to the person
> - the rule in *Wilkinson v Downton*

Intentional interference with the person – trespass

Battery

Battery is the intentional and direct application of unlawful force by one person to another.

Intentional

There does not have to be an intention to commit a harm or battery, there merely has to be an intention to commit the requisite interference with the plaintiff's person. It does have to be an intentional invasion or interference, as opposed to merely negligent.

In *Letang v Cooper* (1965), the plaintiff was sunbathing in the car park of an hotel and the defendant drove his car over her legs injuring her. It was held that the plaintiff could not succeed in trespass, as the defendant's behaviour had been unintentional. The old distinction between trespass and case had been replaced by a distinction between trespass (which lay for intentional, direct invasions of the plaintiff's interest and which was actionable *per se*) and negligence (which lay for all negligent invasions direct or indirect and which was only actionable upon proof of actual injury or damage, *per* Lord Denning).

The general principle is that, to establish an action in trespass, intention must be proved rather than mere negligence.

Direct

The traditional example used to illustrate the difference between direct and indirect harm is that of a man who throws a log onto the highway. If the log strikes someone the injury is direct and trespass would lie but if it simply obstructs the highway and someone trips over it the injury is indirect and the plaintiff would have to sue in negligence and prove damage.

This requirement that the force be 'direct' is clear enough in the example but is not always so easy to draw.

A continuation of the defendant's act will constitute trespass

In *Scott v Shepherd* (1773), a lighted squib was thrown by the defendant, which finally exploded in front of the plaintiff, having been thrown by X and Y, who both acted instinctively for their own preservation. The defendant was liable in trespass as the actions of X and Y had been continuations of his own act. So the act must be direct and therefore it is not battery to poison another's drink, or to dig a hole intending another person to fall in it, even though in each case the intended harm occurs.

Unlawful force

No one can touch someone else without his consent or lawful justification. It seems that only the slightest physical contact is required and no actual hurt need result. In the words of Holt CJ 'the least touching of another in anger is a battery'.

This rule is subject to two possible qualifications:

- Certain forms of contact are considered unavoidable and the generally accepted consequence of social intercourse and therefore not actionable, eg the jostling that takes place in a busy shop or street. All this is reasonable if kept within acceptable bounds. These instances tend to be considered 'implied consent' although in *Collins v Wilcock* (1984) they were regarded as 'falling within a general exception embracing all physical contact which is generally acceptable in the ordinary conduct of daily life'.
- The second qualification stems from the decision of the Court of Appeal in *Wilson v Pringle* (1986). A schoolboy was carrying a bag over his shoulder when another schoolboy pulled at the bag, causing him to fall and suffer injury to his hip. The defendant maintained that it was just an act of horseplay and that the essential ingredients of trespass to the person were a deliberate touching, hostility and an intention to inflict injury. The plaintiff said that there just had to be an intentional application of force.

It was held that an intention to injure was not an essential ingredient of the action for trespass to the person, since it was the mere trespass by itself which was the offence and therefore it was the act rather than the injury which had to be intentional. But the intentional act had to be proved to be a 'hostile touching' which was a question of fact and could not be equated with 'ill will or malevolence'.

Wilson was doubted by Lord Goff (*obiter*) in *F v West Berkshire Area Health Authority* (1989). He argued that a prank that got out of hand, an over-friendly slap on the back or surgical treatment by a surgeon who mistakenly believes that a patient has consented to it may all constitute battery even though there is no element of hostility in the touching. Lord Goff defined battery as any deliberate touching of another's body, beyond the bounds of acceptable everyday conduct, which lacks lawful excuse. This is the preferred view of academic writers.

Lord Goff also suggested that the interest that battery protects is not only freedom from physical injury but also from any form of physical molestation. So it protects against affronts to insult or indignity caused by physical touching. On this basis an unwanted kiss or spitting at the plaintiff can constitute a battery.

Assault

Assault is the act of the defendant which causes the plaintiff reasonable apprehension of the infliction of a battery on him by the defendant.

Relationship of assault and battery

> An assault is an act which causes another person to apprehend the infliction of immediate, unlawful force on his person; a battery is the actual infliction of unlawful force on another person
>
> (*Collins v Wilcock* (1984)).

For example, riding a horse at a person constitutes an assault but riding against him constitutes a battery. Consequently, it is possible for there to be an assault and not a battery. In *Stephens v Myers* (1830), the defendant threatened the plaintiff and moved towards him with a clenched fist but he was prevented from reaching the plaintiff by someone else.

The threat must be sufficient to put the plaintiff in reasonable apprehension of an immediate battery. The plaintiff does not have to show that he was actually frightened. The test is whether it would have been reasonable to apprehend the infliction of a battery. Conversely, there can be a battery without an assault, eg when someone is struck from behind or while asleep.

Where threats of violence or abuse cannot be carried out, then assault cannot be committed, eg in *Thomas v National Union of Mineworkers (South Wales Area)* (1985) there were violent gestures by picketing miners to working miners in passing vehicles but the picketing miners were held back by the police.

Can mere words constitute an assault?

In *Meade's* case (1823), it was 'declared that no words or singing constituted an assault,' but that was said *obiter dicta*. Fleming argues that the highwayman's words 'stand and deliver' would constitute an assault.

It is clear from *Read v Coker* (1753) that threatening words combined with threatening actions is sufficient to constitute an assault.

Words can also negative what would otherwise be an assault. In *Tuberville v Savage* (1669), the defendant did not commit an assault by placing his hand on his sword in the plaintiff's presence because he said the words 'if this was not assize time, I would not take such language from you'. The words spoken had contradicted the defendant's actions.

Must the defendant intend to commit a battery?

Assault used to be thought of as an incomplete form of battery. Therefore, the question arose, if the defendant did not intend to commit battery but nevertheless induced a belief in the plaintiff's mind that he was about to do so would this constitute an assault?

The usual example given is where the defendant points an unloaded gun at the plaintiff. There are conflicting cases on the point but the general consensus of opinion appears to be that it is assault. *R v St George* (1840) (a criminal case) holds that it is an assault; while *Blake v Barnard* (1840) (a civil case) holds that it is not.

It has been said that the analogy between assault and battery cannot be overstated. It has already been shown that battery can take place without prior apprehension of harm by the plaintiff (eg where he is struck from behind) so there is no reason why assault should necessarily be incomplete battery.

Act of assault must be intentional

As with battery the act constituting an assault must be committed intentionally. If negligently done and harm results the appropriate cause of action is in negligence.

Note

Assault and battery are crimes as well as torts and the Offences Against the Persons Act 1861 makes criminal proceedings in certain circumstances a bar to any subsequent civil proceedings, thereby providing against duality of actions. Criminal proceedings can provide an alternative form of compensation, since the court can order the offender to compensate the victim for any personal injury, loss or damage.

Ex gratia payments of compensation may also be made by the Criminal Injuries Compensation Board to victims of crimes.

False imprisonment

This is the infliction of bodily restraint which is not expressly or impliedly authorised by law. Imprisonment in the sense of incarceration is not necessary nor is any use of force. So a person can be lawfully imprisoned in an open field provided his movement is restrained.

The restraint must be complete

If the plaintiff could have left by another route then the restraint is not complete. In *Bird v Jones* (1845), the plaintiff insisted on his right to use part of the highway that had been cordoned off but he was prevented from doing so by the defendant. He was told he could go back the way he had come but could not go straight on. This was not false imprisonment as it was not a total restraint of liberty. Therefore, wherever there is a means of escape, provided that it is reasonable to use it, there will be no false imprisonment. What is a reasonable escape route will depend on the facts of the case.

An occupier of premises is entitled to impose reasonable conditions on the manner in which entrants leave the premises. In *Robinson v Balmain Ferry Co Ltd* (1910), the defendants operated a ferry with turnstiles for payment of the fare on one side of the river. Notices stipulated that a penny must be paid on entering and leaving the wharf. The plaintiff paid to enter but changed his mind about taking the ferry. He then refused to pay another penny to exit the wharf and the defendants prevented him from leaving. This was not false imprisonment. The plaintiff had contracted to leave the wharf by the ferry and the payment of a penny was a reasonable condition on his leaving by another route.

Although the *Robinson* case is not authority for the proposition that there is a general right to detain people to enforce contractual rights, it is clear that it is reasonable in some circumstances to impose conditions as to the point (both in time and in place) of exit, particularly where the plaintiff has by his conduct consented to a state of affairs, eg a passenger on a plane or train, cannot demand to be let off at an unscheduled stop, or while in motion.

In *Herd v Weardale Steel Coal and Coke Co* (1915), the plaintiffs were miners who refused to complete their shift because they considered the work to be dangerous. The defendants' manager refused for some time to allow the lift to be used to take the men up to the lift shaft. The defendants were not in breach of contract because there was no obligation to remove the men except at certain times.

It was held that there was no false imprisonment because the men had voluntarily descended to the mine on the basis that they would be brought to the surface at the end of the shift. They had therefore consented to the action. Also, the defendants had committed no positive act of detention.

This decision tends to indicate that there is no right of action in trespass for a mere omission, although it has been argued that a failure to release miners at the contractually agreed time would have amounted to imprisonment and that liability can be established on the basis of omission. It has also been argued that *Robinson* and *Herd* are not examples of reasonable contractual conditions preventing false imprisonment but instead the plaintiffs had consented to their imprisonment, thereby providing the defendant with a defence.

Must the defendant be aware that he is being falsely imprisoned?

For years there was conflicting authority on this point. In *Herring v Boyle* (1834), a headmaster refused to allow a mother to take her son home for the school holidays because she had not paid the fees for the term. It was held that false imprisonment had not been committed as the boy had been unaware that he had been falsely imprisoned.

By contrast, in the case of *Meering v Grahame-White Aviation Co* (1919), the plaintiff was questioned at the defendant's factory in connection with certain thefts. The plaintiff was unaware that outside the room in which he was being questioned two security men were positioned and would have prevented him from leaving, if necessary.

He succeeded in an action for false imprisonment. Atkin LJ said imprisonment may damage a person's reputation even if he did not know about it. It was somewhat unsatisfactory as an authority as it did not consider *Herring v Boyle* and for that reason can be considered *per incuriam*.

More recently, in *Murray v Ministry of Defence* (1988) the House of Lords approved Atkin LJ's speech in *Meering*. The plaintiff's lack of knowledge was not relevant to the cause of action but to recoverability of damages. If the plaintiff was unaware that he had been falsely imprisoned and had suffered no harm, he could expect to recover nominal damages.

Residual liberty

The House of Lords has held that a prisoner who is lawfully detained in prison pursuant to s 12 of the Prison Act 1952 does not enjoy any 'residual liberty' (*Hague v Deputy Governor of Parkhurst Prison*, *Weldon v Home Office* (1991)). So segregating a prisoner or placing him in a strip cell does not deprive him of liberty which he has not already lost. A prisoner can sue in respect of acts committed against him by fellow prisoners or prison officers acting outside the scope of their authority as those acts fall outside s 12. Alternatively, if a prisoner is held in intolerable conditions he may have a cause of action in negligence.

Excess detention

In the case of *Olotu v Home Office* (1996), the plaintiff was committed for trial to the Crown Court. There was a time limit of 112 days specified in the warrant and she was kept in prison for 81 days in excess of this limit. She sued the Home Office for false imprisonment, arguing that the governor of the prison should have released her after the expiry of 112 days or obtained a further court order. It was held that the governor of the prison did not have the authority to release her without an order from the Crown Court and did not have an independent role in applying for such an order. Although she should have been released on bail, that could only be done by an order of the court. Consequently, the Home Office was not liable. A further attempt to sue the Crown Prosecution Service for beach of statutory duty for failing to bring the plaintiff before the court before the expiry of the time limit also failed (see Chapter 4).

The restraint must be intentional

This is a reflection of the views expressed in *Letang v Cooper*. The tort must also be committed directly. These are requirements of trespass to the person.

If for either reason the plaintiff cannot establish false imprisonment, an action in negligence may still be available.

In *Sayers v Harlow UDC* (1958), the plaintiff became stuck in the defendant's toilet, as a result of faulty maintenance of the door lock by the defendant's servants. In trying to climb out of the toilet, she fell and injured herself. The plaintiff succeeded in negligence but would not have succeeded in false imprisonment because there was no direct act of imprisonment.

Defences to trespass to the person

Once the defendant has proved the direct interference that constitutes trespass, it is for the defendant then to justify his action by reference to one of the defences.

Discipline

The exercise of disciplinary powers remains a defence to an action in tort only in relation to children and in the bizarre case of passengers on board ship.

Apart from cases where injuries inflicted before birth are concerned, children are not prevented from suing their parents even while they remain minors. It is presumed, however, that parents can justify an assault and battery by way of lawful chastisement and correction provided reasonable force is used. Parents can also justify detention of their children when circumstances are justified. The defence extends to those who are *in loco parentis* but it should be noted that s 47 of the Education Act (No 2) 1987 prohibits corporal punishment in state schools and for state funded pupils in independent schools.

The captain of a ship can use reasonable force against anyone who threatens the safety of a ship and it is thought that this defence would apply to the captain of an aeroplane and possibly road and rail transport, as well.

Lawful arrest, search and seizure

Lawful arrest, search and seizure may constitute a defence to false imprisonment, battery or interference with goods.

Arrest with warrant

A policeman who arrests a person under a warrant acts lawfully and commits no trespass.

Arrest without warrant

Section 24 of the Police and Criminal Evidence Act (PACE) 1984 provides for a category of 'arrestable offences', which under s 24(1)–(3) are defined, as follows:

- offence for which the sentence is fixed by law;
- offence punishable with five years' imprisonment or more;

- offences specified in s 24(2) and attempting, conspiring, inciting, aiding, abetting, counselling, or procuring the commission of any of these offences listed in s 24(2).

Under s 24(5), any person may arrest without warrant anyone who is guilty or whom he has reasonable grounds to suspect to be guilty of the offence. This only applies where an arrestable offence has been committed. Where no offence has actually been committed a private individual is not protected from civil liability but under s 24(6) a police officer will be protected provided he had reasonable grounds for the arrest.

Section 24(7) enables a police officer to arrest without warrant anyone who is, or he has reasonable grounds for suspecting to be, about to commit an arrestable offence.

Under s 25, a police officer, in addition to the powers set out in s 24 may effect a lawful arrest where the 'general arrest conditions' set out in s 25 are satisfied:

- where a constable has reasonable grounds for suspecting that any non arrestable offence is being, or has been, committed or attempted and it appears to him that service of summons is impracticable and any of the general arrest conditions are satisfied;
- name and address are unknown or believed to be unreliable;
- arrest is necessary to prevent physical injury, damage to property, offence against public decency or obstruction of the highway;
- constable has reasonable grounds for believing that arrest is necessary to protect a child or other person.

The manner of arrest

Section 28 of the PACE 1984 stipulates the basic rules governing the manner of a lawful arrest. An arrested person must be told as soon as practicable both that he is under arrest and what the grounds of arrest are. Section 28 largely enacts the common law rules delivered in the judgment in *Christie v Leachinsky* (1947).

Private citizens effecting an arrest must, as soon as is reasonable, hand the arrested person over to the police. They cannot detain suspects on their own premises or embark upon their own investigations. This does not mean that the police must be summoned immediately as can be seen from the case of *John Lewis & Co Ltd v Timms* (1952) when the plaintiff was arrested by the defendant's store detectives. She was held for some 20 to 60 minutes while the manager decided whether or not to call the police. This delay was held to be reasonable in the circumstances.

Section 30(1) of the PACE 1984 provides that a constable arresting a person must take him as soon as is practicable to the police station.

Necessity

One may lawfully protect one's person and property and that of another against the threat of harm even though the consequence is that an innocent person suffers loss.

In *Leigh v Gladstone* (1909), a suffragette prisoner who was fasting to death was forcibly fed through the mouth and nose by prison officers; she sued them for battery. It was held that it was a good defence that forcible feeding had saved her life. Recent cases have made it clear that outside prison, medical patients can refuse treatment even if that results in their risking death but the situation with regard to prisoners is unclear.

In *F v West Berkshire Area Health Authority* (1989), the House of Lords relied on the defence of necessity as justifying sterilisation of a 36-year-old woman who was a voluntary patient in a mental hospital and had the mental age of five and was therefore under a permanent incapacity. The House of Lords preferred to rely on necessity rather than rely on an implied form of consent and was prepared to allow all treatment that was given in the 'best interests' of the patient and would be endorsed by a reasonable body of medical opinion. This is criticised by Jones in *Textbook on Torts* (4th edn) as it gives the medical profession wide powers to determine the extent of the defence. Doctors should seek a declaration from the court before giving treatment but such a declaration is not mandatory for adult patients (Lord Griffiths dissenting).

The case highlighted a gap in the law in relation to mental patients. The Mental Health Act 1983 dispenses with the need to obtain consent with respect to psychiatric treatment for patients formally detained in a mental hospital but it does not enable anyone to give consent to treatment for someone under a mental incapacity who is a voluntary patient or for physical treatment for detained patients. The Law Commission is currently reviewing this area.

It was also said that the defence of necessity would authorise medical treatment to a patient who is temporarily unconscious and unable to give consent in order to save the patient's life and prevent permanent damage to health. Lord Brandon said that not only would it be lawful for doctors to intervene in this way but it would also be their 'common law duty to do so'.

Consent

Conduct which would otherwise constitute trespass to the person may be rendered not actionable because of express or implied consent.

Sport

Participants in a sport where physical contact is part and parcel of the game impliedly consent to contacts that occur within the rules of the game and even certain forms of contact that are not permitted under the rules. A sportsman does not consent to force which could not reasonably be expected to happen in the course of the game.

In *R v Billinghurst* (1978), there was a deliberate punch at a player who did not have the ball and this constituted a battery. Similarly, in *McNamara v Duncan* (1979), a deliberate contact with a player who does not have the ball in football, constitutes a battery.

Consent to medical treatment

Any physical contact with a patient by a doctor without his patient's consent constitutes *prima facie* a battery. However, the patient's consent need not be in writing and will often be inferred/implied from conduct. Before surgery patients tend to be asked to sign a consent form which declares the 'effect and nature' of the treatment have been explained. In order for the consent to be effective, the doctor must have advised the patient in broad terms of the procedure. A failure to warn the patient of the risks or side effects of treatment will not vitiate the consent, where this happens the appropriate form in action is in negligence against the doctor for breach of his duty to give proper and skilled advice (*Sidaway v Bethlem Royal Hospital Govrs* (1985)).

A conscious and competent adult can do what he likes with his own body and is able to refuse medical treatment. Therefore, in *Malette v Shulman* (1991), a doctor who gave a blood transfusion to a Jehovah's witness committed a battery.

However, if someone exercising authority over the plaintiff has exercised undue influence, then this will invalidate the refusal. In *Re T* (1992), the patient who needed a blood transfusion but had been persuaded by her mother, a Jehovah's witness, to refuse such treatment when in a weakened condition, had not validly given refusal.

Recently, the Court of Appeal has held in *Re MB* (1997) that where a woman has capacity, she has the right to refuse a Caesarean section, even if it means the death of the baby. An irrational decision does not amount to incompetence. The test is whether there is 'some impairment or disturbance of mental dysfunctioning' rendering the woman incapable of making a decision. On the facts of the case, a fear of the anaesthetist's needle made the woman incompetent to decide for herself.

Minors

Section 8(1) of the Family Law Reform Act 1969 stipulates that a minor over 16 may effectively consent to surgical, medical or dental treatment. Where a child is under 16, the common law provides that where the individual is mature enough to make up his own decision on the treatment proposed, the child can give effective consent.

In *Gillick v West Norfolk and Wisbech Area Health Authority* (1986), the plaintiff failed in her action to ensure that the contraceptive pill could not be prescribed to her daughter without her consent. The House of Lords held that a doctor when faced with a request for the pill or an abortion from a young girl should first urge the child to discuss the matter with her parents. If this fails, then he may lawfully prescribe it provided he is satisfied that the girl has sufficient understanding of the treatment and its implications. Where a child is too young to give consent then parental consent to treatment will be effective.

It was held in *Re T (a minor)* (1996) that where a parent refuses consent to life-saving invasive surgery, the paramount consideration in deciding whether leave should be granted was the welfare of the child. Although there was a 'very strong presumption in favour of a course of action that will prolong life', prolonging life is not the sole objective of the court and to require it at the expense of other considerations may not be in the child's best interests. On the facts of the case, leave was not granted. The mother was opposed to the surgery and consequently it was not in the child's best interest to force the mother to cope with the consequences of major surgery.

Defence of person or property

A person may use reasonable force to protect his person or property from attack. The defendant must prove:

- that it was reasonable in the circumstances to defend himself; and
- that the force used by him was reasonable.

So, in *Cockcroft v Smith* (1705), the Clerk of the Court sued an attorney for biting off his forefinger in a scuffle. It was no defence that the plaintiff had first run his fingers towards the defendant's eyes. For in the words of Holt CJ a man must not 'in case of a small assault, give a violent or unreasonable return'.

It is also possible to defend those with whom one is in a close relationship such as spouse, child and employer. A distinction used to be made between these classes of people and the defending of a stranger for which there was no defence. However, these distinctions are now thought to be obsolete and that it is now possible to defend anyone from unlawful force providing reasonable force is used.

It is also possible to use reasonable force to prevent a trespass onto land or to eject a trespasser. This right only extends to the occupier or the occupier's agent. The trespasser must first be asked to leave and a reasonable opportunity given for him to do so. The force must be no more than is necessary to ensure that the trespasser leaves the land.

In *Revill v Newberry* (1995), a case decided in negligence, it was held that the defendant had used greater force than was justified in self-defence when he fired a shotgun through a hole in a door and hit a trespasser.

Statutory authority

Statutes may authorise the defendant to commit what would otherwise be a tort. For example, blood tests under ss 20–23 of the Family Law Reform Act 1969 would constitute a battery in the absence of statutory authority.

Contributory negligence

Contributory negligence is a defence to trespass to the person.

Intentional physical harm other than trespass

A wilful act (or statement) of the defendant calculated to cause harm to the plaintiff and in fact causing him harm is a tort.

The rule originated in *Bird v Holbrook* (1828) which established liability for intentionally causing harm which has been inflicted indirectly. It cannot be considered trespass as the harm arises indirectly. For all practical purposes, it is classified alongside trespass to the person in textbooks.

The principle was applied in the case of *Wilkinson v Downton* (1897). The defendant, as a joke, told the plaintiff that her husband had been involved in an accident and that she was to take two pillows and a cab to the scene of the accident, to take him home. The plaintiff suffered severe nervous shock as a result. The defendant was liable for this behaviour that was intended to cause harm.

A similar case was that of *Janvier v Sweeny* (1919) where the plaintiff received damages from the defendants when they told her a false story that she was wanted by the police for correspondence with a German spy.

The rule in *Wilkinson v Downton* remained dormant until the last few years and is now enjoying something of a revival. It has been used to plug a gap in domestic violence law. There is no legislation which covers violence between couples who are not husband and wife or who live in the same household as husband and wife. Couples who are in a close relationship such as homosexuals, mother and son or a couple in a sexual relationship who have not lived together cannot rely on the Domestic Violence and Matrimonial Proceedings Act to obtain a non-molestation order but must instead seek an injunction in tort. However, pestering or harassment is not always tortious. In *Burnett v George* (1992), the Court of Appeal held that a plaintiff who has suffered abuse which endangers health will succeed under *Wilkinson v Downton*. Assault, unwelcome visits and harassing telephone calls were acts calculated to cause harm. This has been called a new tort of 'personal injury by molestation' by Fricker [1992] Fam Law 158.

6 Torts relating to land

You should be familiar with the following areas:
Private and public nuisance

- the difference between public nuisance and private nuisance
- definition of private nuisance
- the distinction between physical damage and amenity damage
- the circumstances taken into account in assessing amenity damage
- whether fault is required for private nuisance
- defences to private nuisance
- situations which have been held not to constitute a defence in private nuisance
- remedies for private nuisance

Rule in *Rylands v Fletcher*

- rule of strict liability – liability in the absence of fault
- non-natural user
- meaning of escape
- whether personal injuries are recoverable
- whether the plaintiff needs to have a proprietary interest
- nature of the accumulation
- meaning of something likely to do mischief
- defences
- remoteness
- future of strict liability for hazardous activities

Fire

- liability at common law
- defences to the action at common law
- Fire Prevention (Metropolis) Act 1774
- interpretation of Fire Prevention (Metropolis) Act 1774, so as to exclude negligently started fires
- development of other rights of action which create liability for fire
- *dicta* of Mackenna J in *Mason v Levy Auto Parts of England Ltd* (1967)

Private nuisance

The relationship between private nuisance and public nuisance

There tends to be confusion between public and private nuisance. Public nuisance is a crime covering a number of interferences with rights of the public at large such as brothel keeping, selling impure food and obstructing public highways. It is not tortious unless an individual proves that he has suffered particular damage beyond that suffered by the rest of the community.

Private nuisance is an unlawful interference with the use or enjoyment of land or some right over, or in connection with it. However, the recent landmark case of *Khorasandjian v Bush* (1993) seems to allow the tort of nuisance to be used to restrain activities which do not affect enjoyment of the plaintiff's land. The plaintiff was granted an injunction not only in respect of harassing telephone calls at home but also for harassment at work or in the street.

Private nuisance has also been held to extend to damage to a floating barge moored in a river (*Crown River Cruises Ltd v Kimbolton Fireworks Ltd* (1996)). Since the barge was in use as a mooring it was so attached for the purpose of the better use and enjoyment of the plaintiffs' mooring right and therefore sufficient to sustain an action for private nuisance.

Public nuisance is different from private nuisance as it is not necessarily connected with the user of land. Public nuisance is usually a crime although it can be a tort. To make matters even more confusing the same incident can be both a public and a private nuisance.

Types of private nuisance

Private nuisance is an unlawful interference with the use or enjoyment of land, or some right over or in connection with it. What is unlawful falls to be decided in an *ex post facto* manner. Most activities which give rise to claims in nuisance are in themselves lawful. It is only when the activity interferes with another's enjoyment of land to an extent that it is a nuisance that it becomes unlawful.

Examples of private nuisance

It was said by Lord Wright that 'the forms that nuisance take are protean'. Examples would be as follows:

- encroachment on the plaintiff's land (*Davey v Harrow Corporation* (1958));

- physical damage to the plaintiff's land (*Sedleigh-Denfield v O'Callaghan* (1940));
- interference with the plaintiff's use or enjoyment of land through smells, smoke, dust, noise, etc (*Halsey v Esso Petroleum Co Ltd* (1961));
- interference with an easement or *profit*.

Physical damage

As a general rule, nuisance is not actionable *per se* and actual damage must be proved, subject to the following exceptions:

- where a presumption of damage can be made, eg where a building is erected so that one of the cornices projects over the land of the plaintiff, it may be presumed that damage will be caused to the land of the plaintiff by rain water dripping from the cornice onto the land;
- interference with an easement;
- *profit à prendre*; or
- right of access where there has been acquiescence in certain circumstances.

So, private nuisance is concerned with balancing the competing claims of neighbours to use their property as they think fit. However, a distinction must be made between physical damage to property, where such conduct will, subject to the *de minimis* rule, be a nuisance and personal discomfort or amenity damage, where the judge will consider many factors to determine the balance.

If the conduct complained of causes physical damage to the plaintiff's property, this will amount to nuisance (subject to any defence available). In *St Helens Smelting Co v Tipping* (1865), Lord Westbury said an 'occupier is entitled to expect protection from physical damage no matter where he lives'.

Amenity damage

Amenity damage is interference such as noise, smells, dust and vibrations which will interfere with use and enjoyment of land without physically damaging the property.

In the case of amenity damage, the degree of interference has to be measured against the surrounding circumstances. These factors are as follows:

Nature of the locality

This is an important determinant of what constitutes nuisance in the case of amenity damage. As was said in *St Helens Smelting Co v Tipping*

(1865) 'one should not expect the clean air of the Lake District in an industrial town such as St Helens'. The plaintiff's estate was located in a manufacturing area. Fumes from a copper smelting works damaged the trees on the estate. The distinction was made between physical and damage and amenity damage, particularly the nature of the surrounding area and locality.

Interesting questions of locality were raised in *Halsey v Esso Petroleum Co* (1961). The plaintiff's house was in a zone that was classified as residential for planning purposes. The defendant's oil depot was across the road in an industrial zone.

There was a combination of physical and amenity damage:

- acid smuts from the defendant's depot damaged paintwork on the plaintiff's car, clothing and washing on the line and there was a nauseating smell;
- noise from the boilers caused the plaintiff's windows and doors to vibrate and prevented him from sleeping and there was also noise from the delivery tankers at night.

The damage to the clothing on washing line etc constituted physical damage and was recoverable. Before allowing recovery for the intangible damage, the locality had to be taken into account. Trifling inconveniences were disregarded but the locality set the measure of what was acceptable and the interference substantially exceeded the standards of the surrounding neighbourhood.

In *Laws v Florinplace Ltd* (1981), the defendants opened a sex centre and cinema club which showed explicit sex acts. Local residents sought an injunction. It was held that the use constituted a private nuisance.

Similarly, in *Thompson-Schwab v Costaki* (1956), the plaintiff lived in a respectable residential street in the West End of London. The defendant used a house in the same street for the purposes of prostitution. It was held that having regard to the character of the neighbourhood the defendant's use of the property constituted a nuisance.

In the public nuisance case of *Gillingham v Medway (Chatham) Dock Co* (1992), it was held that the nature of a locality can be changed through planning permission.

However, it should be noted that in the *Gillingham* case, the nature of the locality had changed. It was held in *Wheeler v JJ Saunders Ltd* (1995) that grants of planning permission to intensify pig farming on a site already used for that purpose did not render the grantees immune from liability in nuisance for the smells caused by the implementation of those planning permissions.

Abnormal sensitivity

Personal discomfort is not to be judged by the standards of the plaintiff but must be made by reference to the standards of any ordinary person who might occupy the plaintiff's property. It must be an 'inconvenience materially interfering with the ordinary comfort physically of human existence, not merely according to elegant and dainty modes and habits of living but according to plain and sober and simple notions among the English people' *per* Knight Bruce VC in *Walter v Selfe* (1851).

Consequently, a vicar who was put off his sermons in *Heath v Mayor of Brighton* (1908) by a low hum from the defendant's electricity works was being abnormally sensitive particularly as he had been the only person annoyed and it had not stopped anyone from attending church.

Abnormal sensitivity and physical damage

In the same way that a defendant will not be liable for physical damage to property caused because of its exceptionally delicate nature. A man cannot increase the liabilities of his neighbour by applying his own property to special uses.

In *Robinson v Kilvert* (1889), the plaintiff occupied a basement in the ground floor of the defendant's building and stored brown paper there. The defendant's boiler had an adverse effect on the plaintiff's goods, although it would not have effected any other type of paper. The plaintiff failed to get an injunction because of the exceptionally delicate trade that he was carrying on.

Interference with television signals

In *Bridlington Relay Ltd v Yorks Electricity Board* (1965), the plaintiffs were in the business of relaying sound and television broadcasts and the defendant's power lines interfered with their transmissions. It was held that the plaintiffs were carrying on an exceptionally delicate trade.

Interference with television signals was again held by the House of Lords to be an actionable nuisance in *Hunter v Canary Wharf* (1997). The presence of Canary Wharf tower interfered with the plaintiffs' television reception but they did not succeed in private nuisance.

Substantial interference

On the other hand, if the defendant's activities would have interfered with the ordinary use of the land, he will be liable notwithstanding the plaintiff's abnormal sensitivity. In *McKinnon Industries Ltd v Walker* (1951) the Privy Council held that once substantial interference is proved, the remedies for interference will extend to a sensitive and delicate operation.

Duration of interference

Interference of a temporary or occasional nature, may cause annoyance, but an injunction will rarely be granted. The temporary duration of the alleged nuisance is one factor to be taken into account and the judge will conclude that it is the price of social existence that neighbours suffer temporary annoyance at various times, such as during building or renovation.

The defendant in *Swaine v GN Railway* (1864) dumped refuse next to the plaintiff's property before moving it onto another property. The plaintiff's claim in nuisance failed as it was temporary and occasional.

Grave temporary interference

The courts will allow actions for temporary nuisance where the interference is grave. So, in *Matania v National Provincial Bank* (1936) the plaintiff succeeded when a temporary nuisance, in the form of building works carried on by the defendant's independent contractors, prevented the plaintiff from carrying on his livelihood, as a music teacher.

Similarly, in *De Keyser's Royal Hotel v Spicer Bros* (1914), use of a steam pile driving machine outside the plaintiff's hotel causing hotel guests to lose a night's sleep and the prevention of after dinner speakers from making themselves heard also constituted nuisance.

Single act of the defendant

Nuisance is usually associated with a continuing state of affairs rather than a single act of the defendant. It was held in *British Celanese Ltd v AH Hunt (Capacitors) Ltd* (1969) that an isolated occurrence could constitute nuisance.

In *SCM (UK) Ltd v WJ Whittall & Son Ltd* (1970), it was said that for a single escape to constitute nuisance, the nuisance had to arise from the condition of the defendant's land. It should be remembered that a single occurrence could constitute a right of action under the rule in *Rylands v Fletcher*.

Malice

Motive is generally irrelevant in tort, as can be seen from *Bradford Corporation v Pickles* (1895) where a bad motive on its own did not create a right of action. This rule needs qualification in the case of private nuisance, as malice may tip the scales in the defendant's favour, and conduct which would not otherwise be actionable becomes unlawful and a nuisance if it has been committed maliciously. In *Christie v Davey* (1893) the defendant lived next door to a music teacher. He objected to the noise and retaliated with banging on the walls, beating trays, etc. The plaintiff was granted an injunction but the outcome would have been different if the acts had been innocent.

In *Hollywood Silver Fox Farm Ltd v Emmett* (1936), the plaintiffs bred silver foxes. If they are disturbed in the breeding season they eat their young. The defendant fired a gun as near as possible to the breeding pens with the malicious intention of causing damage. The defendant was held liable although the decision has been criticised on the grounds that breeding silver foxes was an exceptionally delicate trade. It seems that the element of malice was sufficient to alter the outcome.

Public benefit

It is not a defence in nuisance to say that the activity is being carried on in the public benefit (*Adams v Ursell* (1913)). Nevertheless, if the activity is being carried out for the good of the community in general, then the courts are more likely to find the use of the land to be reasonable.

Defendant's negligence

The fact that a defendant has acted with all reasonable care does not necessarily mean that the use of the land was reasonable. On the other hand, want of reasonable care may be strong evidence of a nuisance. It is not reasonable to expect a plaintiff to endure discomfort that the defendant could have avoided with reasonable care.

Lord Reid in *The Wagon Mound (No 2)* (1967) said that '... negligence in the narrow sense may not be necessary, but fault of some kind is almost always necessary, and generally involves foreseeability'.

As nuisance is a tort which relates to user of land, fault in nuisance is thought to relate to unreasonable use of land. This makes fault in nuisance an altogether more subjective concept than in negligence. Nuisance does not use the same concepts for assessing fault as negligence. For example, it does not require the existence of a duty of care before establishing the existence of fault but confusingly, judges have used the terminology of negligence when discussing nuisance. Nuisance protects a wider range of interests than negligence. The latter is mainly concerned with physical interests whereas the former protects against noise, smells, dust, etc and will compensate for pure commercial losses (*Campbell v Paddington Borough Council* (1911)).

Nuisance is also distinct from negligence in terms of who has *locus standi* to bring an action and the remedies available.

Liability has been imposed in public nuisance in the absence of fault (*Tarry v Ashton, Wringe v Cohen*).

Who can sue?

Nuisance protects those persons who have an interest in the land affected, so only an owner or occupier can sue. Until recently, a person who did not have a proprietary interest in the land could sue.

95

In *Malone v Laskey* (1907), the wife of a licensee whose enjoyment of the land was interfered with could not sue in nuisance, as she did not have a proprietary interest.

The recent case of *Khorasandjian v Bush* (1993) has added a new twist to the tale, as no proprietary interest was required from the plaintiff, who was the owner's daughter. The Court of Appeal relied on the Canadian case of *Motherwell v Motherwell* (1977), where *Malone v Laskey* was distinguished since the plaintiff was the spouse of a licensee. If she had been the spouse of a tenant then she would have succeeded. Clement JA talked of the distinction between one who is 'merely present' and 'occupancy of a substantial nature'.

In *Hunter v Canary Wharf* (1995), Pill LJ held that a substantial link between the person enjoying the use and the land was essential but occupation of the property, as a home, conferred on the occupant a capacity to sue in private nuisance. However, when the case reached the House of Lords, *Khorasandjian v Bush* was overruled and a mere licensee can no longer sue in private nuisance.

Who can be sued?

The creator of the nuisance

A person who creates a nuisance by positive conduct may be sued. It is not necessary for the creator of the nuisance to have any interest in the land from which the nuisance emanates.

In the words of Devlin J in *Southport Corporation v Esso* (1953): 'I can see no reason why ... if the defendant as a licensee or trespasser misuses someone else's land he should not be liable for a nuisance in the same way as an adjoining occupier would be.'

The occupier

The occupier is the usual defendant in private nuisance. An occupier will be liable for:

Persons under his control
Under the principles of agency and vicarious liability.

Independent contractors
Where nuisance is an inevitable or foreseeable consequence of work undertaken by independent contractors, the occupier cannot avoid liability by employing a contractor as has been already seen in the case of *Matania v National Provincial Bank Ltd* (1936).

Actions of a predecessor in title

An occupier who knows or ought reasonably to have known of the existence of a nuisance created by a predecessor in title will be liable for continuing the nuisance if he does not abate it. If the nuisance could not reasonably have been discovered he will not be liable.

It was held in *St Anne's Well Brewery Co v Roberts* (1929) that if at the date of a letting, the landlord knows or ought to know of the condition giving rise to the actionable nuisance, then he is liable during the tenancy where he does not take from the tenant a covenant to repair.

Actions of trespassers

An occupier is not liable for a nuisance created on his land by a trespasser unless he adopts or continues the nuisance.

In *Sedleigh-Denfield v O'Callaghan* (1940), the boundary between the appellant's premises and the respondents' was a hedge and a ditch, both of which belonged to the respondents. Without informing the respondents a trespasser laid a pipe in the ditch and some three years later the pipe became blocked and the appellant's garden was flooded. The respondents' servants had cleared the ditch out twice yearly. The appellants claimed damages in nuisance.

It was held that he would succeed because the respondents knew or ought to have known of the existence of the nuisance and permitted it to continue without taking prompt and efficient action to abate it.

Acts of nature

At common law, it was thought that an occupier had no duty to abate a nuisance that arose on his land from natural causes. The extent of the obligation was to permit his neighbour access to abate the nuisance. The Privy Council in *Goldman v Hargrave* (1967) established that an occupier is under a duty to do what is reasonable in the circumstances to prevent or minimise a known risk of damage to the neighbour's property.

The appellant was the owner/occupier of land next to the respondents. A tree on the appellant's land was struck by lightning and caught fire. The appellants took steps to deal with the burning tree but subsequently left the fire to burn itself out and took no steps to prevent the fire spreading. The fire later revived and spread causing extensive damage to the respondent's land. The appellants were held to be liable.

In *Leakey v National Trust* (1980), the defendants owned a hill that was liable to crack and slip. The plaintiffs owned houses at the foot of the hill. After a large fall the plaintiffs asked the defendants to remove the earth and debris from their land but they refused saying they were not responsible for what had occurred. The defendants were held liable in nuisance. It was reasonable to prevent or minimise the known risk of damage or injury to one's neighbour or to his property.

In *Bradburn v Lindsay* (1983), it was held that where houses have mutual rights of support, negligently allowing property to fall into dereliction so as to damage the adjoining premises is actionable in negligence as well as in nuisance.

The landlord

A landlord may be liable for a nuisance arising in three types of situation:

- where the landlord authorised the nuisance;

  In *Sampson v Hodson-Pressinger* (1981), a tiled terrace was built over the plaintiff's sitting room and bedroom. The noise was excessive and it was held that the landlord was liable in nuisance.

- where nuisance existed before the date of the letting;
- where the landlord has an obligation or right to repair.

Defences

Prescription

A defendant who has carried on an activity for 20 years may claim a prescriptive right to commit the nuisance. The activity must be an actionable nuisance for the entire 20-year period.

In *Sturges v Bridgman* (1879), a confectioner and a physician lived next door to each other. The confectioner used two large machines and had done so for more than 20 years. The noise and vibrations had been no problem until the physician built a consulting room at the end of his garden. It was held that the confectioner could not rely on the defence of prescription as there was no actionable nuisance until the consulting room had been built.

Statutory authority

If a statute authorises the defendants' activity the defendants will not be liable for interferences which are inevitable and could not have been avoided by the exercise of reasonable care.

In *Allen v Gulf Oil Refining Ltd* (1981), a statute authorised the defendants to carry out oil refinement works. The plaintiff complained of noise, smell and vibration. It was held that the defendants had a defence of statutory immunity.

It is *not* a defence to plead that:

- The defendant moved to the nuisance (*Sturges v Bridgman; Miller v Jackson* (1977)). Cricket had been played on a village ground since 1905. In 1970, houses built in such a place that cricket balls went into a garden. It was held that there was a nuisance that was an interference with the reasonable enjoyment of land. It was no defence to say the defendant had brought trouble onto his own head by moving there.
- That there is a substantial public benefit. In *Adams v Ursell* (1913), the defendant ran a fish and chip shop. The plaintiff objected to the noise and smells. The defendant tried to argue that the fish and chip shop was of public benefit but it was held that this was no defence.
- That the nuisance is the result of the separate actions of several people. In *Pride of Derby & Derbyshire Angling Association Ltd v British Celanese Ltd* (1952), pollutant sewage from factories reached a river through the effluent pipe of a local authority from the sewage works. It was held that the local authority were responsible.

Remedies

- Damages
- Injunction
  An injunction is an equitable, and therefore a discretionary, remedy. If the injunction is a continuing one, the plaintiff will be granted an injunction except:
  (a) if the injury to the plaintiff's legal rights is small
  (b) is one capable of being estimated in money
  (c) is one adequately compensated by a small money payment
  (d) is a case where it would be oppressive to the defendants to grant an injunction
- Abatement or self-help
  Notice should be given except in an emergency or where it is not necessary to enter the wrongdoer's land.
In *Co-operative Wholesale Society Limited v British Railways Board* (1995), it was held that the right to abatement was confined to cases where the security of lives and property required immediate and speedy action or where such action could be exercised simply without recourse to the expense and inconvenience of legal proceedings in circumstances unlikely to give rise to argument or dispute. Where an application to court could be made, the remedy of self-help was neither appropriate or desirable.

Public nuisance

A public nuisance is a crime as well as a tort. The remedy for a public nuisance is a prosecution or relator action by the Attorney General on behalf of the public. A plaintiff who suffers particular damage, over and above the damage suffered by the rest of the public may maintain an action in public nuisance. Public nuisance has been defined by Romer LJ in *AG v PYA Quarries Ltd* (1957) as 'an act or omission which materially affects the reasonable comfort of a class of Her Majesty's subjects'.

The distinction between public and private nuisance

Public nuisance

- protects land and other interests;
- primarily a crime;
- plaintiff must prove special damage over and above the rest of the public;
- single act can be enough;
- no defence of prescription;
- exemplary damages are not available;
- strict liability for some forms of highway damage.

Private nuisance

- essentially protects land;
- only a tort;
- plaintiff must prove damage;
- for single act it is necessary to show it arose from state of affairs;
- prescription is a defence;
- exemplary damages may be available;
- fault must usually be proved subject to exceptions.

Public nuisance is most important in relation to highways

What obstructions are actionable?
A temporary or permanent obstruction that is reasonable in amount and duration will not be a nuisance.

In *R v Russell* (1805), the defendant left wagons standing on the street for several hours at a time for the purpose of loading and unloading and this was held to be a public nuisance.

In *AG v Gastonia Coaches Ltd* (1977), overnight parking in the street of coaches constituted a nuisance.

An obstruction which creates a foreseeable danger will amount to a nuisance.

In *Ware v Garston Haulage Co* (1944), an unlit vehicle parked at night so as to obstruct the highway, may cause a nuisance, although it will depend on the facts.

In *Dymond v Pearce* (1972), the defendant parked a lorry overnight under a lit street lamp without lights. This was regarded as a nuisance although the plaintiff did not succeed as the nuisance was not the cause of the plaintiff's injury. While in *Dollman v Hillman* (1941) a piece of fat on which someone slipped was a nuisance.

Premises adjoining the highway

Tarry v Ashton (1876) is an example of public nuisance being a tort of strict liability, in certain cases. The defendant's lamp projected over the highway. An independent contractor repaired the lamp but it fell on the plaintiff; the defendant was found liable in the absence of fault.

Similarly, in *Wringe v Cohen* (1939), a wall to the defendant's houses which were let to weekly tenants collapsed but the defendants were liable to keep the house in a good state of repair. The defendants did not know that the wall was in a dangerous condition but were nevertheless held to be liable. In *Mint v Good* (1951), again a wall in front of houses which were let to weekly tenants collapsed although there was no express agreement between the landlord and tenant as to repair. The landlord was held to be liable.

Does the occupier have to be aware of the nuisance?

In the recent case of *R v Shorrock* (1993), the defendant let a farm on his field to three persons for a weekend for £2,000. The defendant did not know the purpose for which the field had been let. The field was used for an acid house party lasting 15 hours and attended by between 3,000 and 5,000 people who paid £15 per person admission. Many local people complained about the noise and disturbance caused by the party and the defendant and the organisers were charged with public nuisance. It was held that it was not necessary to show that the defendant had actual knowledge of the nuisance but merely that he knew or ought to have known the consequences of activities carried out on his land.

The defendant ought to have known that there was a real risk that the consequences of the licence would create the nuisance that occurred.

Particular damage

The plaintiff must suffer direct and substantial damage to bring an action in public nuisance.

The following have been held to be special damage:

- additional transport costs, caused by an obstruction (*Rose v Miles* (1815));
- obstructing access to a coffee shop (*Benjamin v Storr* (1874));
- obstructing the view of a procession so that the plaintiff lost profit on renting a room (*Campbell v Paddington Borough Council* (1911)).

The rule in *Rylands v Fletcher*

The rule in *Rylands v Fletcher* is a rule of strict liability, ie it does not require proof of negligence or lack of care, or wrongful intention, on the part of the defendant. However, actual damage must be proved; it is not a tort that is actionable *per se*.

The original statement

The rule was originally formulated by Blackburn J in *Rylands v Fletcher* in the following terms 'the person who for his own purposes brings onto his land, and collects or keeps there, anything likely to do mischief if it escapes, must keep it in at his own peril and, if he does not do so, is *prima facie* answerable for all the damage which is the natural consequence of the escape'. This was approved by the House of Lords and the condition that there must be a 'non-natural user' was added by Lord Cairns.

Limits of the rule

These may be summarised as follows:

- there must have been an *escape* of something 'likely to do mischief';
- there must have been a *non-natural use* of the land.

There must be an escape

In *Read v Lyons & Co Ltd* (1947), it was said that escape, for the purposes of applying the proposition in *Rylands v Fletcher*, means (*per* Lord Simon) 'escape from a place where the defendant has occupation or control over land to a place which is outside his occupation or control' and (*per* Lord Macmillan) 'there must be the escape of something from one man's close to another man's close'.

In *Read v Lyons*, the plaintiff was a munitions worker who was injured by an exploding shell while in the defendant's munitions factory. It was held that there had not been an escape of a dangerous thing, so the defendant could not be liable under *Rylands v Fletcher*.

The plaintiff must prove not only that there has been an escape but that damage is a natural consequence of the escape.

Can a plaintiff sue for personal injuries?

There is some controversy as to what type of damage is recoverable under *Rylands v Fletcher*. In *Read v Lyons Co Ltd*, it was questioned whether *Rylands v Fletcher* could be used for personal injuries claims, particularly by Lord Macmillan. Nevertheless, it is now generally accepted that an occupier would be able to maintain an action for personal injuries.

In *Hale v Jennings* (1938), a 'chair o plane' from a fairground attraction became detached and landed on the plaintiff's stall, on an adjoining ground. A claim for personal injuries was allowed. Such a claim was also allowed in *Miles v Forest Rock Granite Co Ltd* (1918).

In *Perry v Kendrick's Transport* (1956), it was said that the plaintiff could recover for personal injuries even where he had no interest in the land affected.

However, the rule in *Rylands v Fletcher* will not extend so far as to cover situations where a plaintiff has no interest in the land which is affected by the escape, and whose only loss is financial (*Weller v FMDRI* (1966)).

Does the plaintiff have to be an occupier?

There is a dispute as to whether or not it is necessary to have an interest in the land in order to maintain an action under the rule in *Rylands v Fletcher*.

While there are comments in such cases as *Read v Lyons* and *Weller v FMDRI* which seem to suggest that the plaintiff must be an occupier or have some interest in the land, there are other cases which adopt a broader view. Lawton J said *obiter* in *British Celanese v Hunt* (1969) that the plaintiff need not be the occupier of adjoining land, or any land. Furthermore, it was held that to use the premises for manufacturing was an ordinary use of the land. The issue can only be settled by the House of Lords. An authoritative decision on this point is required.

Non-natural user

This requirement was added by Lord Cairns in the House of Lords in *Rylands v Fletcher* itself. This expression is highly flexible and enables the court to take into account their own interpretation of contemporaneous needs. The way the Privy Council expressed the position in *Rickards v Lothian* (1913) emphasised the flexibility:

> It must be some special use bringing with it increased danger to others and must not merely be the ordinary use of the land or such a use as is proper for the general benefit of the community.

There have, however, been decided cases which have maintained that certain circumstances can confidently be regarded as being outside the sphere of *Rylands v Fletcher* because the courts have held that the land is being naturally used, eg lighting of a fire in a fire place (*Sochacki v Sas* (1947)); storing metal foil strips in a factory (*British Celanese v Hunt* (1969)).

In deciding what constitutes a natural use, Lord Porter in *Read v Lyons* said: '... each seems to be a question of fact subject to a ruling by the judge as to whether ... the particular use can be non-natural and in deciding this question I think that all the circumstances of the time and place and practice of mankind must be taken into consideration so what might be regarded as ... non-natural may vary according to the circumstances.'

For example, storage of motor parts and engines in *Mason v Levy Auto Parts* (1967) was not a natural use having regard to the large quantities of combustible material, manner of storage and character of the neighbourhood.

Non-natural use is a flexible concept and will vary according to time and context. For example, in *Perry v Kendricks Transport* (1956), the Court of Appeal found itself bound by the decision of *Musgrove v Pandelis* (1919) in holding that a full tank of petrol was a non-natural use of the land. Some commentators maintain that this would not be applied today.

Storage of chemicals for industrial use in large quantities was held to be a non-natural use in *Cambridge Water Co Ltd v Eastern Counties Leather plc* (1994).

'Brings onto his land and keeps there'

The thing may or may not be something which in its nature is capable of being naturally there. What matters is whether the particular thing has in fact been accumulated there. *Rylands v Fletcher* only applies to things artificially brought or kept upon the defendant's land.

There is no liability for things naturally on the land, such as the spread of thistles from ploughed land in *Giles v Walker* (1890) or rocks falling from a natural outcrop in *Pontardawe RDC v Moore-Gwyn* (1929).

These cases can be contrasted with *Crowhurst v Amersham Burial Board* (1878) where yew trees planted close to railings spread onto an adjoining meadow on which the plaintiff pastured his horse, which was poisoned and died as a result of eating yew leaves. The defendant was liable, although the yew trees were capable of being naturally there, the defendant had planted the trees and therefore they constituted an accumulation.

Liability in negligence and nuisance

The old common law rule was that an occupier was not under a duty to abate a nuisance that arises from his land as a result of natural causes. This was changed by the Privy Council in *Goldman v Hargrave* (1967) and was applied by the Court of Appeal in *Leakey v National Trust for Places of Historic Interest or Natural Beauty* (1980). The remedy for an escape of something occurring naturally on the land is, therefore, in nuisance or negligence not under *Rylands v Fletcher*.

'Anything likely to do mischief if it escapes'

This is a question of fact in each case. However, things which have been held to be within the rule include electricity, gas which was likely to pollute water supplies, explosives, fumes and water.

A very broad view can be taken. In *AG v Corke* (1933), it was held that the owner of land who allowed caravan dwellers to live on it was answerable for the interference they caused on adjoining land, on the basis that they were 'things likely to do mischief'.

Defences

Consent of plaintiff

If the plaintiff has permitted the accumulation of the thing which escapes, then he cannot sue. Implied consent, such as common benefit is also a defence.

Common benefit

If the accumulation benefits both the plaintiff and the defendant, this is an important element in deciding whether the plaintiff is deemed to have consented.

In *Carstairs v Taylor* (1871), rainwater which had been collected on the roof of a block of flats for the benefit of several occupants meant that the landlord was not liable when the water escaped as it had been accumulated for a common benefit. While in *Peters v Prince of Wales Theatre* (1943) a fire extinguisher which exploded damaging part of the building occupied by the plaintiffs was also held to have been accumulated for a common benefit.

Blackburn J spoke only of persons who 'for his own purposes' brings something onto his land. Thus, gas, water, electricity boards and inland waterways authorities carrying out statutory duties do not accumulate for their own purposes, so *Rylands v Fletcher* does not apply.

Act of a stranger

It is a defence that the escape was caused by the unforeseeable act of a stranger over whom the defendant has no control.

In *Rickards v Lothian* (1913), someone deliberately blocked a basin in the defendant's premises and turned the taps on, flooding the plaintiff's premises below. While in *Perry v Kendricks Transport* (1956) the plaintiff was injured by an explosion caused by a boy trespasser who threw a lighted match into a petrol tank. The Court of Appeal held that the defendants were not liable as they had no control over trespassers and had not been negligent.

Foreseeable act of a stranger

The defendant in *Hale v Jennings* (1938) ought reasonably to have foreseen the act of a third party and had enough control over the premises to prevent the escape.

Act of God

If an escape is caused, through natural causes and without human intervention, in 'circumstances which no human foresight can provide against and of which human prudence is not bound to recognise the possibility' (*Tennent v Earl of Glasgow* (1864)), then there is said to be the defence of Act of God.

In *Nichols v Marsland* (1876), the defence succeeded where a violent thunderstorm caused flooding.

The case was put into proper perspective by the House of Lords in *Greenock Corporation v Caledonian Railway Company* (1917) where an extraordinary and unprecedented rainfall was held in similar circumstances not to be an Act of God. The explanation of *Nichols v Marsland* (1876) was that there the jury found that no reasonable person could have anticipated the storm and the court would not disturb a finding of fact.

Earthquakes and tornadoes may sometimes be Acts of God but few other phenomena seem likely to be within the scope of *Rylands v Fletcher*.

Statutory authority

Sometimes public bodies storing water, gas, electricity and the like are by statute exempted from liability so long as they have taken reasonable care. It is a question of statutory interpretation whether, and, if so, to what extent, liability under *Rylands v Fletcher* is excluded.

Liability was excluded in *Green v Chelsea Waterworks Co* (1894) when, without negligence on the defendants' part, their water main exploded and flooded the plaintiff's premises.

This can be compared to *Charing Cross Elec Co v Hydraulic Power Co* (1914) where the defendants were liable when their hydraulic main burst even though there was no question of negligence on their part, as the statute did not exempt them from liability.

Default of the plaintiff

The defendant is not liable where damage is caused by the plaintiff's act or default. If the plaintiff is partially responsible then the Law Reform (Contributory Negligence) Act 1945 will apply.

In *Ponting v Noakes* (1894), the defendant's colt reached over the defendant's land and ate some branches of a yew tree and died. The action did not succeed as the animal's death was due to its wrongful intrusion.

Where the damage is attributable to the extra sensitivity of the plaintiff's property then there is no liability (*Eastern & South African Telegraph Co Ltd v Cape Town Tramways Co Ltd* (1902)).

Remoteness

Blackburn J said that a defendant is *prima facie* liable for all the damage which is the natural consequence of the escape.

It was argued that following the decision of the Privy Council in *The Wagon Mound (No 2)* (1967) that the test for remoteness of damage is foreseeability then the test in *Rylands v Fletcher* is also foreseeability.

It has also been argued that where damage has been caused as a result of the extraordinary risk created by the defendant then the defendant should be liable for the unforeseeable risk.

An important development has been the House of Lords' decision in *Cambridge Water Co Ltd v Eastern Counties Leather plc* (1994). It was held that foreseeability of damage was an essential prerequisite of liability. Strict liability arises only if the defendant knows or ought to foresee that the thing which is stored might cause damage if it escapes. Once there is such knowledge or foreseeability, the defendant is liable even if he takes all reasonable care to prevent the escape.

Future of strict liability for hazardous activities

The scope of the rule in *Rylands v Fletcher* has been cut down considerably by the requirements that there be a non-natural use of the land.

The defences, particularly act of a stranger and statutory authority, turn a tort of strict liability into an inquisition on the defendant's culpability.

The Pearson Commission recommended a statutory scheme of strict liability for personal injuries resulting from exceptional risks. Under the scheme strict liability would be imposed in two circumstances:

- those which by their unusually hazardous activities require close, careful supervision; and
- those which, although normally safe, are likely to cause serious and extensive casualties if they do go wrong.

Contributory negligence and voluntary assumption of the risk would be general defences but statutory authority and act of a third party would not. The fact that the plaintiff was a trespasser would not be a general defence but could be introduced as a defence to a specific type of exceptional risk when making the statutory instrument.

Fire

Liability at common law

Liability was originally established for fire in *Beaulieu v Finglam* (1401). The writ in that case used the expression *tan negligenter ac improvide*. The defendant had 'kept his fire that it escaped'. 'Negligence' means negligence in its old, not modern, sense. If the defendant started a fire on his land which spread, he would be liable. The duty imposed on occupiers was a strict one. The occupier was liable for fires started by his guests, servants and independent contractors.

The occupier was not liable for fires started by strangers or acts of God.

'Stranger'

This was originally limited to trespassers. In *Beaulieu v Finglam* (1401), it was said that the occupier was not liable if the fire was caused 'by a man outside my household'. This was confirmed in *Tuberville v Stamp* (1697) when Holt CJ said that if: 'A stranger sets fire to my house and burns my neighbour's house, no action will lie against me.'

Lord Denning in *H and N Emanuel Ltd v Greater London Council* (1971) extended the defence by allowing it to apply to guests in certain circumstances: 'A stranger is anyone who in lighting a fire or allowing it to escape acts contrary to anything which the occupier of the house could anticipate that he would do.'

Prior to this, it has always been thought that the occupier would be liable for fires started by guests but according to this *dictum* an occupier would not be liable for a fire started by a guest if the guest's conduct in lighting the fire was so alien to the invitation then with regard to the fire then he ought to be regarded as a trespasser.

Centuries later other remedies became available for starting a fire under the rule in *Rylands v Fletcher*, nuisance and negligence.

Fire Prevention (Metropolis) Act 1774

This Act still applies and s 86 provides:

> No action, suit or process whatsoever shall be had, maintained or prosecuted against any person in whose house, chamber, stable, barn or other building, or on whose estate any fire shall *accidentally* begin.

This cut down the effect of the common law rule for fire, since the occupier would no longer be liable for accidental fires. However, in

Filliter v Phippard (1847), it was held that a fire did not start 'accidentally' within the meaning of the Act when it started 'negligently'. A fire only started accidentally when it started by 'mere chance' or 'was incapable of being traced to any cause'.

Also, the Act does not apply where a fire does start accidentally but is negligently allowed to spread. As in *Musgrove v Pandelis* (1919) when a fire started 'accidentally' in the defendant's car. The fire could have been stopped if the defendant had turned off the tap connecting the petrol tank with the carburettor. He did not do so and the fire spread to the plaintiff's flat causing damage. The defendant was liable as the spread of the fire was regarded as a second fire which had not started 'accidentally'.

Immunity under the statute is illustrated by the following cases:

- *Collingwood v Home and Colonial Stores Ltd* (1936)
  A fire broke out because of defective electrical wiring on the defendant's premises, without negligence on the defendant's part.

- *Sochacki v Sas* (1947)
  A fire was properly lit and a spark jumped out of it causing it to spread.

- *Spicer v Smee* (1946)
  This case is authority for the proposition that fire can be actionable under nuisance.

Strict liability for fire and *Rylands v Fletcher*

The rule of strict liability for fire laid down in *Beaulieu v Finglam* predated that in *Rylands v Fletcher*.

In *Musgrove v Pandelis,* a car kept in a garage attached to a house, which contains a tank full of petrol was held to be a 'non-natural' use of the land and also something likely to do 'mischief' if it escapes. It was held that the rule in *Rylands v Fletcher* applied. Bankes LJ said that the Fire Prevention (Metropolis) Act 1774 was not intended to apply to *Rylands v Fletcher* type situations. This was said even despite the fact that *Rylands v Fletcher* did not exist at the time of the Act!

The findings in *Musgrove v Pandelis* have been severely criticised and doubted. If it is correct then the rule of strict liability for fire has now been subsumed into *Rylands v Fletcher*.

Mackenna J criticised the decision in *Mason v Levy Auto Parts of England Ltd* (1967). He said that liability for fire could not be based on the rule in *Rylands v Fletcher*. He argued that the car had not escaped from the land in *Musgrove v Pandelis* nor had the petrol in the tank.

Liability for fire should have arisen under the old common law principles laid down in *Filliter v Phippard*. *Rylands v Fletcher* was not the same as these principles but had developed out of them.

The test, Mackenna J said, was that the defendant must have brought onto the land something likely to catch fire and must have kept the thing on the land in such conditions that if they did ignite the fire would spread to the plaintiff's land and the thing brought onto the land was in the course of some non-natural use and the thing ignited and spread.

He uses very similar language to that used by Blackburn J in *Rylands v Fletcher* but there is a subtle but very real difference.

Under *Rylands* the thing itself escapes. Under Mackenna J's test the defendant would have to bring inflammable material onto his land which then sets alight and spreads to the neighbouring land. This seems a more logical test since under *Rylands* the defendant would have to bring fire onto his land and the fire would have to escape. The *Mason* test says that the defendant would have to bring something onto his land which is likely to catch fire and if the fire starts it would spread to neighbouring land.

Liability under statute

Legislation has been passed with respect to fires started by sparks from railway engines. Where statute has authorised the use of a railway line by engines, liability could not be imposed by the railway line owners for fires caused by sparks from the engine, if the owners had not been negligent.

In *Vaughan v Taff Vale Railway Co* (1860), sparks from an engine belonging to the defendants set fire to a wood owned by the plaintiff. The defendants had been authorised by statute to use the railway and had taken every precaution. The railway company was liable.

This can be contrasted with *Jones v Ffestiniog Railway Co* (1868), where the railway owners were liable as they did not have statutory authority.

The rule was thought to be hard on farmers so the Railway Fires Acts of 1905 and 1923 were passed which created liability for fires caused by sparks from trains but limited the liability to £200 in respect of damage to land and crops.

Trespass to land

Trespass to land has been defined by Winfield and Jolowicz as 'the unjustifiable interference with the possession of land'. Since it is a form of trespass it is actionable *per se*. The interest it protects is the plaintiff's interest in the peaceful enjoyment of his property. It therefore protects possession not ownership. Consequently, the plaintiff must be in possession of the land.

Trespass to land will only help the lessor, if there is damage to the reversion (*Jones v Llanrwst UDC* (1911)).

Nor will trespass to land protect a licensee such as a lodger or guest (*Hill v Tupper* (1863); *Allan v Liverpool Overseers* (1874)).

The court will look for possession in fact, not possession in law, it is possible to be temporarily absent from the house, eg on an errand.

A lessee is regarded as having possession for the purpose of trespass (*Graham v Peat* (1801)).

Nature of the interference

The interference must be direct and immediate. The most common example would be entering on the plaintiff's land without permission.

However, the tort is very varied and can be committed in many different ways. Placing a ladder against a wall can be trespass (*Westripp v Baldock* (1938)).

A person who has permission to be on the land can become a trespasser if they abuse their permission or remain on the land after the permission has been withdrawn (*Robson v Hallett* (1967)).

Trespass can be 'continuing', when it takes place over a period of time. When it is continuing it gives rise to a new cause of action from day to day, as long as the trespass lasts.

Particular forms of trespass

Trespass on the highway

The highway is used for travelling from one point to another. Trespass will be committed when the highway is used for some purpose which is not incidental to the purpose of passage.

In *Hickman v Maisey* (1900), the defendant walked back and forth along the same stretch of highway studying the form of racehorses which were practising nearby. This constituted trespass.

In *Harrison v Duke of Rutland* (1893), the defendant opened and closed an umbrella to frighten pheasants away from the plaintiff's land. This also constituted trespass.

Trespass to the subsoil

Trespass need not be committed against the surface of the land itself, it can be committed against the subsoil (*Cox v Moulsey* (1848)).

Trespass to airspace

The old common law rule was that trespass could not be committed to airspace (*Pickering v Rudd* (1815)).

This was rejected in *Kelsen v Imperial Tobacco Co Ltd* (1957). In this case, an advertising sign was overhanging the defendant's property by eighth inches; this constituted trespass.

The intrusion must be of a height to interfere with the plaintiff's use of the property (*Lord Bernstein of Leigh v Skyviews and General Ltd* (1978)). The plaintiff had objected to aircraft flying over his property and taking aerial photographs. It was held that there was no interference with the plaintiff's property.

The rule was restricted in *Anchor Brewhouse Developments Ltd v Berkley House (Docklands Development) Ltd* (1987). Here, booms from a crane were overhanging the defendant's property. It was said that the rule in *Bernstein* did not apply to static structures.

Trespass *ab initio*

Where a defendant's entry is with the authority of the law and the defendant subsequently abuses that right he becomes a trespasser *ab initio* from the moment he enters onto the plaintiff's land.

In *Chic Fashions (West Wales) Ltd v Jones* (1968), the police entered the plaintiff's premises with a warrant. They seized goods not mentioned in the warrant but it was held that they were not trespassers as they had general authority to look for stolen goods.

Nature of the interference

Trespass is a tort of intention but there is High Court authority that trespass to land can be committed negligently. In *League Against Cruel Sports v Scott* (1985), the defendants had been forbidden from allowing their foxhounds to enter onto the land of the plaintiff. The defendant had unintentionally been responsible for his hounds trespassing onto the plaintiff's land and was liable in trespass.

Defences

Licence
Where the defendant's licence has been revoked by the plaintiff he has a reasonable time to leave the premises (*Robson v Hallett*).

A contractual licence can only be invoked in accordance with the terms in the licence (*Hurst v Picture Theatres Ltd* (1915)).

Lawful authority
Examples would include entering pursuant to a right of way or exercise of powers under the Police and Criminal Evidence Act 1984.

Necessity
It is a defence to show it was necessary to enter onto the plaintiff's land. In *Rigby v Chief Constable of Northamptonshire* (1985), the police fired a CS gas cylinder into a building to flush out a psychopath who was sheltering there. The defence was applicable but the plaintiff was awarded damages as the police were negligent in firing the equipment without fire fighting equipment.

Remedies

Damages
Where the trespass is minimal, damages will be nominal. Where there is damage, the measure of damages will be the diminution in the value of the land. Aggravated or exemplary damages will be awarded where appropriate.

Injunction
Where the trespass is continuing the plaintiff is *prima facie* entitled to an injunction. Where a trespass is threatened but not yet committed then the plaintiff may seek an injunction.

Re-entry
A person who is entitled to possession may re-enter the land and use reasonable force. Forcible re-entry is a criminal offence under s 6 of the Criminal Law Act 1977.

Mesne profits
The plaintiff may claim for profits which the defendant has obtained from his occupation of the property, damages for deterioration of the property and reasonable costs of obtaining possession.

Ejection

A right to ejection only exists where there is an immediate right to enter the property.

Distress damage feasant

If a chattel is unlawfully on the plaintiff's land and has done actual damage to the plaintiff's property, the plaintiff may retain the property until the owner pays, or offers to pay, compensation for the damage done.

The remedy of distress damage feasant was not available to a defendant who had clamped a plaintiff's car in *Arthur v Anker* (1995). The object of the remedy was to take prompt action to stop or prevent damage to the land or anything on it. Actual damage to the user of the land had to be shown and the chattel was retained as security for a claim to be compensated. From the facts of the case, it was clear that the leaseholders had not suffered any damage. There was a flat charge to be released from the clamp. It was the same charge, regardless of the duration of the trespass and it was not paid to the leaseholders but to the agents who fitted the clamp. The defendants did, however, have the defence of consent (see Chapter 8).

7 Defamation

> **You should be familiar with the following areas:**
>
> - the difference between libel and slander
> - the test for defamatory statements
> - situations when slander is actionable *per se*
> - essentials for defamation
> - the role of judge and jury
> - defences to defamation
> - proposals for reform

Examples of defamatory statements

Defamation may take the form of the mere physical relationship of objects. In *Monson v Tussauds Ltd* (1894), the defendants placed an effigy of the plaintiff, against whom a charge of murder was 'not proven', close to those of convicted murderers. It was held to be *prima facie* libel, although an injunction was not granted.

In *Youssoupoff v MGM* (1934), the defendants implied, in a film, that Princess Youssoupoff had been raped by Rasputin. This was held to be a libel, on the basis that to say a woman had been raped would tend to make her shunned and avoided, even though she is morally blameless.

'Right thinking members of society'

The test for defamation is whether the plaintiff would be lowered in the eyes of right thinking members of society. In *Byrne v Dean* (1937), it was alleged that a lampoon was defamatory because it accused the plaintiff of 'sneaking' to the police about unlawful gambling in his club. The action of the club committee in allowing the lampoon to remain on the notice board did not constitute defamation since members of society would not be right thinking if they thought it defamatory to say that a man had discharged his public duty to help suppress crime.

The difference between libel and slander

Libel is the written or permanent form of defamation. Slander is the spoken or otherwise transient form.

Libel	Slander
Permanent	Temporary

See also s 1 of the Defamation Act 1996; ss 4 and 7 of the Theatres Act 1968

Actionable *per se*	Not actionable *per se*, subject to exceptions
May also be a crime	Never a crime unless blasphemous

What constitutes special damage?

Some actual loss, the loss of some material or temporal advantage which is pecuniary or capable of being estimated in money, eg the loss or refusal of an office or employment or the dismissal from a situation, the loss of a client or dealing.

As a special rule, slander is not actionable *per se*. However, there are exceptions:

Criminal offence

Where the words impute a crime for which the plaintiff can be made to suffer physically by way of punishment. The crime concerned does not have to be an indictable one but it has to be one which the plaintiff could be punished with imprisonment in the first instance.

The words 'you are a convicted person' were found to mean that a crime punishable corporally was imputed in *Gray v Jones* (1939), since although they would not place the plaintiff in jeopardy, they would cause him to be ostracised socially.

The general feeling behind the exception is the social ostracism that would result from such a slander.

Disease

Where the words impute to the plaintiff a contagious or infectious disease, then that is a form of slander actionable *per se*. Decided cases have held that leprosy, venereal disease and perhaps the plague come within this exception. However, it must be contagious or infectious – an oral imputation of insanity is not actionable without proof of special damage (unless it comes within one of the other exceptions).

It was held in *Bloodworth v Gray* (1844) that to infer that a person has a contagious venereal disease is to commit slander *per se*.

Unchastity of a woman

By s 1 of the Slander of Women Act 1891, where the words impute adultery or unchastity to a woman or girl.

Incompetence

Where the words are calculated to disparage the plaintiff in any office, profession, calling, trade or business held or carried on by him at the time of publication under s 2 of the Defamation Act 1952.

Who can sue?

The tort of defamation protects an individual's interest in his reputation. It was suggested by the Faulks Committee that the purpose of the law of defamation is to strike a balance between a person's interest in their reputation and the general right of free speech.

It was in the interests of free speech that the House of Lords overruled the decision in *Bognor Regis Urban District Council v Campion* (1972) in *Derbyshire County Council v Times Newspapers Ltd* (1993). The former case held that a local authority had an interest in its governing reputation, whereas the latter held that if local authorities could sue in defamation then that would inhibit free speech. In the Court of Appeal, reliance had been placed on Article 10 of the European Convention of Human Rights (despite the fact that the Convention has not been incorporated into English law) but the House of Lords relied on a common law principle of free speech.

A trading corporation can sue in defamation in order to protect its commercial reputation (*Metropolitan Saloon Omnibus Co v Hawkins* (1859)).

A trade union used to be able to sue in defamation but s 2(1) of the Trade Union and Labour Relations Act 1974 deprives a trade union of the right to incorporated status with the result that it lacks the necessary legal personality.

A person can only bring a defamation action during their lifetime and the right does not survive for the benefit of the deceased's estate.

Legal aid is not available for a defamation action. This has lead to it being called a rich man's tort. It was held in *Joyce v Sengupta* (1993) that the plaintiff can bring an alternative cause of action, for which legal aid would be available, in this case malicious falsehood, even though the defendant would then be deprived of the right to jury trial.

Essentials of defamation

The plaintiff has to prove the following in order to establish the existence of defamation:

- that the statement was defamatory;
- that the statement referred to the plaintiff;
- that the statement was published.

The words must be defamatory

Words can be defamatory in a wide variety of situations. In *Sim v Stretch* (1936), the defendant sent a telegram to the plaintiff, stating 'Edith has resumed her position with us today. Please send her possessions and the money you borrowed, also her wages ...'. In an action for libel, the plaintiff argued that the words of the telegram were defamatory, as they suggested that, out of necessity, he had borrowed money from the housemaid and that he had failed to pay her wages. The test applied was 'would the words lower the plaintiff in the eyes of right thinking members of society?' The claim failed as the words were not capable of a defamatory meaning.

The test was also applied in *Byrne v Dean* with the result, again, that the defendant was not liable, as right thinking members of society would report illegal activities to the police. So it could not be defamatory to suggest that someone had done so.

Different problems arose in *Tolley v Fry* (1931). The plaintiff was a leading amateur golfer. Without his knowledge or consent, the defendants issued an advertisement showing the plaintiff playing golf with a packet of chocolate in his pocket. The plaintiff felt that this compromised his amateur status and he brought an action for libel alleging that the advertisement meant that the plaintiff had, for gain and reward, agreed to its publication. It was held to be defamatory.

What constitutes defamation should be distinguished from mere vulgar abuse which may injure someone's dignity but not their reputation.

In *Penfold v Westcote* (1806), the words 'you blackguard, rascal, scoundrel, Penfold, you are a thief' were a mixture of both defamation and abuse. 'Blackguard' etc was abuse but was defamatory in conjunction with the word 'thief'.

The plaintiff in *Field v Davis* (1955) had been called 'a tramp', which was held capable of a defamatory meaning but on the facts of the case and the plaintiff's temper when he made the remarks they was obviously meant as vulgar abuse.

Function of judge and jury

It is the judge's function to decide as a matter of law whether the statement is reasonably capable of bearing the defamatory meaning alleged by the plaintiff. If he is not satisfied then he withdraws the case from the jury.

The jury's function is to decide as a matter of fact whether the statement complained of is defamatory, in that particular case.

In *Lewis v Daily Telegraph* (1963) the defendants printed articles stating that the Fraud Squad were inquiring into the affairs of the plaintiff. It was alleged that the words were defamatory on their ordinary and natural meaning. On appeal, it was held that the judge should have ruled whether the words were capable of bearing the defamatory meaning put forward and that the jury should have been directed that they could have not meant this meaning.

Since the case of *John v MGN Ltd* (1995), the judge also provides guidance to libel juries in their role of assessing compensatory damages. The judge may make reference to an appropriate figure, which would compensate the plaintiff, or to brackets of awards. In addition, the judge may make reference to conventional personal injury awards which acts as a check on the reasonableness of the awards that the jury is proposing to make.

It was also held that it was for the judge to set down limits to the possible range of meanings which could be inferred from words complained of as being defamatory and for the jury to decide the actual meaning within that range (*Mapp v News Group Newspapers Ltd* (1997)).

Juries do not hear and determine cases under the offer to make amends procedure contained in ss 2–4 of the Defamation Act 1996 nor under the fast track procedure under ss 8–10 of the Defamation Act 1996.

Determining the meaning of the words complained of

The plaintiff may complain of the natural and ordinary meaning of the words (*Lewis v Daily Telegraph*).

Natural and ordinary meaning

The natural and ordinary meaning is that which is conveyed to the ordinary, reasonable and fair-minded reader. The jury must decide a single meaning that would be conveyed to such a reader and cannot divide readers into different groups, with some groups inferring different meanings to others.

These principles were recently upheld by the House of Lords in *Charleston v News Group Newspapers Ltd* (1995). The plaintiffs played a respectable married couple in the Australian soap opera *Neighbours*. Photographs of their faces had been superimposed onto photographs of two near naked bodies, apparently engaging in an obscene act. There was an additional photograph of the female plaintiff superimposed onto a photograph of a topless woman. Above the photographs was a headline which read: 'Strewth! What's Harold up to with our Madge?' Below the photographs was a smaller headline which stated: 'Porn Shocker for *Neighbours* Stars.' The text of the article which followed made it clear that the faces had been superimposed by the makers of a computer game, without the plaintiffs' knowledge or consent. The article roundly condemned the makers of the computer game. Readers of the entire article would have known that the plaintiffs had not consented to the photographs but they argued that those reading only the headlines would have drawn a different inference. The idea that readers could be divided into different groups, with these groups inferring different meanings was rejected.

Guidelines to the meaning to be attributed to particular words was provided by Neill LJ in *Gillick v BBC* (1995) (following Sir Thomas Bingham MR in *Skuse v Granada Television* (1993)), as follows:

- the natural and ordinary meaning was that conveyed to the ordinary reasonable viewer/reader;
- the hypothetical reader or viewer was not naive but he was not unduly suspicious. He could indulge in loose thinking and could read in an implication more readily than a lawyer. But he was not avid for scandal and did not select one bad meaning when other non-defamatory meanings were available;
- the court should be cautious of over-elaborate analysis;
- the reasonable viewer/reader would not give the analytical attention that a lawyer would to a document, an auditor to the interpretation of accounts or an academic to the content of a learned article;

- the court were entitled to have regard to the impression made;
- the court should not be too literal in its approach;
- a statement was defamatory if it lowered people in the eyes of right thinking members of society.

The word spoken by a participant in a discussion on a live television programme that, 'there were at least two reported cases of suicide by girls who were pregnant' after the success of a legal action brought by a campaigner opposed to giving contraceptive advice to girls, were capable of bearing the defamatory meaning that the campaigner was morally responsible for the deaths. However, note now the statutory defence contained in s 1 of the Defamation Act 1996. This provides, *inter alia*, that a broadcaster of a live programme containing a statement in circumstances in which he has no effective control over the maker of a statement has a statutory defence.

It was held by the Court of Appeal in *Botham v Khan* (1996) that in deciding whether an alleged libel was capable of bearing a particular meaning, the important point was what the defendant said the plaintiff had done, not what the defendant thought was the true quality of the act. The defendant had alleged that the plaintiff had been involved in ball tampering in cricket, which was contrary to the rules. He went on to state that he did not consider it cheating. The important point was that the plaintiff had been accused of cheating and it did not make any difference that in the defendant's opinion it was not considered to be cheating. The words were capable of being defamatory and it was for the jury to decide.

The plaintiff must normally give details of the meanings he ascribes to the words complained of. Where a plaintiff relies on the ordinary meaning of words but those words have more than one ordinary meaning, or have acquired a meaning outside their common or dictionary definitions, it is desirable and may be necessary, for the plaintiff to give particulars of all the meanings inherent in the words.

In *Allsop v Church of England Newspaper* (1976), the plaintiff was a well-known broadcaster and claimed damages from the defendants for having twice referred to his 'preoccupation with the bent', within the context of pornography, violence, sex and obscenity on the screen. The plaintiff relied on the ordinary meaning of the words and there was no plea of innuendo.

It was held that the word 'bent' was used as slang in a context that made its meaning imprecise and the plaintiff had to give particulars of every meaning he felt was inherent in the words. This would apply even if 'true' or 'false' innuendo or even the 'natural and ordinary meaning' of the words is relied on.

Innuendo

An apparently innocent statement may nevertheless be defamatory if it contains an innuendo. So, the plaintiff may claim that the words are defamatory in the light of external facts and circumstances known to persons seeing/ hearing the words – the innuendo.

An innuendo must be specially pleaded, ie the plaintiff must state the grounds (with supporting evidence, eg his special knowledge) on which he alleges that the apparently innocent remark is defamatory, ie he must prove the meaning that he alleges to the words.

An innuendo may arise, not from the words but from the facts and circumstances surrounding the publication. In *Cassidy v Daily Mirror* (1929), under the heading 'Today's Gossip' the *Daily Mirror* published a photograph of the plaintiff's husband and a certain Miss X 'whose engagement has been announced'. The defendants maintained that they had received the photograph in the ordinary course of business and had published in good faith. The plaintiff was living apart from her husband and alleged that the words were defamatory since the innuendo was that she was not married to her husband.

It was held that the publication could be defamatory and since the jury found that the caption conveyed to reasonably minded people an aspersion on the plaintiff's moral character; she was entitled to succeed.

It is not necessary to show, however, that anyone having knowledge of the extrinsic facts and seeing or hearing the words would actually understand them as defamatory. It was held in *Hough v London Express* (1940) that the 'fact of defamation' refers to the defamatory meaning of the words, not their effect on the plaintiff's reputation because it is irrelevant that the statement is not believed to be true by anyone to whom it is published.

It is not necessary to show that the defendant knew of the extrinsic facts which made the words defamatory, as in *Cassidy v Daily Mirror*. However, ss 2–4 of the Defamation Act 1996 provides a defence of making amends through an 'offer of amends'.

The words must refer to the plaintiff

If the plaintiff is mentioned by name, there is usually no difficulty about this and furthermore there is no requirement that the defendant should have intended to refer to the plaintiff.

In *Hulton v Jones* (1908), the plaintiffs were newspaper proprietors and published in their newspaper a humourous account of a motor festival in Dieppe in which imputations were cast on the morals of Artemus Jones, a church warden at Peckham. This person was believed by the writers of the article to be fictitious. In fact, there was a barrister named Artemus Jones who was not a churchwarden, did not live in Peckham and had taken no part in the Dieppe festival.

He sued the defendants for libel and friends swore that they believed that the article referred to the plaintiff. The plaintiff succeeded and it was immaterial that the defendants did not intend to defame him. In the words of an American judge, the question is not who it aimed at but who is hit.

In the case of *Newstead v London Express* (1939), the Court of Appeal carried *Hulton v Jones* further in two directions.

They held that:

- the principle applies where the statement truly relates to a real person, A, and is mistakenly but reasonably thought to refer to another real person, B; and
- absence of negligence on the defendant's part is relevant only in the sense that it may be considered by the jury in determining whether reasonable people would regard the statement as referring to the plaintiff, otherwise it is no defence.

In the *Newstead* case, the statement was 'Harold Newstead, 30-year-old Camberwell man' has been convicted of bigamy. This was true of a Camberwell barman of that name but it was untrue of the plaintiff, Harold Newstead aged about 30 who helped his father in a hairdressing business in Camberwell. The defendants were liable, although it must be remembered that if the case was heard today the defence under s 4 of the Defamation Act 1996 would be available.

Material may be defamatory of the plaintiff even where it does not refer to him by name and even if it contains no 'key or pointer' indicating that it refers to him.

In *Morgan v Odhams Press* (1971), a newspaper article alleged that a girl had been kidnapped by a dog-doping gang. At the relevant time the girl had been staying at the plaintiff's flat and the plaintiff produced six witnesses who swore that they believed that the article referred to the plaintiff. The House of Lords held that these facts constituted sufficient material to leave to the jury.

The test of whether the words 'refer to the plaintiff' is whether the hypothetical, sensible reader having knowledge of the special circumstances would believe that the plaintiff was referred to and due allowance must be made for the fact that such a reader will not give a sensational article in a popular newspaper the attention a lawyer would bestow on a perusal of evidence. Nor is it relevant that the person who actually read the defamatory article believed it to be true.

Class defamation

The question whether an individual can sue in respect of words which are directed against a group, body or class of persons generally was considered by the House of Lords in *Knupffer v London Express Newspapers Ltd* (1944).

It was held:

- The crucial question was whether the words were published 'of the plaintiff' in the sense that he can be said to be personally pointed at rather than the application of any arbitrary general rule that liability cannot arise from words published of a class.
- Normally where the defamatory statement is directed to a class of persons no individual belonging to the class of persons is entitled to say that the words were written or spoken of himself.

Thus, a class cannot be defamed as a class nor can an individual be defamed by general reference to the class to which he belongs.

The plaintiff must show that he was personally pointed at and where words are directed at a class, no individual will be able to rely on an action unless the class is so limited that words apply to each member as an individual.

The words must be published

Publication means the communication of words to at least one other person, other than the person defamed. For there to be injury to the plaintiff's reputation communication to the plaintiff himself is not enough. In *Huth v Huth* (1914), the defamatory material was in an unsealed letter sent through the post and the letter was opened and read by an inquisitive butler. As it was no part of his duty to do this, there was no publication for which the defendant was responsible. Although the defendant had been unwise in not sealing the envelope, the butler's behaviour was not a direct consequence of sending the letter.

The situation will be different where the defendant can reasonably anticipate that someone other than the plaintiff will open the envelope, even where the letter is addressed to the plaintiff. In *Theaker v Richardson* (1962), the defendant wrote to the plaintiff accusing her of shoplifting, being 'a very dirty whore' and a 'lying, low-down brothel-keeping whore and thief'. He put it in a manilla envelope, which he addressed to the plaintiff and put it through her letter box. Her husband opened it thinking that it was an election address. The plaintiff succeeded and on appeal, it was held that there was a finding of fact by the jury which could not be disturbed.

Husband and wife situations

Communication of defamatory material by a husband to his wife or *vice versa*, is *not* a publication for the purposes of defamation. However, if someone wrote to the husband about the wife or *vice versa* that would be defamation.

Repetition

Every repetition of defamatory words is a fresh publication and creates a fresh cause of action. Furthermore, where a libel is contained in a television programme or newspaper article there is a separate publication to every person who read the newspaper or saw the programme, though in practice the plaintiff will normally sue in respect of the edition or broadcast.

A distinction is made between a mere distributor and a person who takes an active part in the production of the print.

Romer LJ set down some guidelines in *Vizetelly v Mudie's Select Library* (1900) which seems to determine when a distributor would be liable. Basically, the distributor will be able to claim a good defence if they can prove:

(a) that they were innocent of any knowledge of the libel contained in the work; and

(b) that there was nothing in the work or in the circumstances in which it came to them or was disseminated by them which ought to have led them to suppose that it contained a libel; and

(c) that when the work was disseminated by them, it was not by any negligence on their part that they did not know that it contained a libel.

In the later case of *Sun Life v WH Smith* (1934), Scrutton LJ felt that (b) and (c) might be combined into a single question 'ought the defendant to have known that the matter was defamatory', ie was it due to his negligence in conducting his business that he did not know?

In *Vizetelly's* case, the proprietors of a circulating library were held liable because they took no steps to ascertain whether their books contained libels and had overlooked a publisher's request for return of copies of the particular book.

Section 1 of the Defamation Act 1996 creates a new statutory defence for distributors, printers, Internet providers, broadcasters of a live programme concerning statements where the broadcaster has no effective control over the maker of the statement and others. This defence supersedes the old common law defence of 'innocent dissemination'. The defence is available to a person if he shows that he was not the author, editor or publisher of the statement complained of, he took reasonable care in relation to his publication, and he did not know and had no reason to believe, that what he did caused or contributed to the publication of a defamatory statement. Regard shall be had to the extent of his responsibility for the content of the statement or decision to publish it; the nature or circumstances of the publication and the previous conduct or character of the author, editor or publisher.

A repetition of a defamatory statement is normally too remote for the defendant to be responsible for it, however, there must be a break in the chain of causation. In *Slipper v BBC* (1991), the plaintiff argued that damages should be increased to take cognisance of the fact that the defendant had invited press reviews of the film which repeated the defamation. The Court of Appeal held that republication was an aspect of *novus actus interveniens* and it was arguable that the defendants could reasonably foresee and anticipate as a natural and probable consequence that the sting of the libel would be repeated in the national press. It was a question of fact for the jury to decide whether the defendant invited such reviews.

Assent to publication

If the plaintiff expressly or impliedly assents to the publication of matter which is true on the face of it, the defendant is not liable and this is so even if it appears that some persons may interpret the statement in a sense much more prejudicial to the plaintiff than is warranted by the plain meaning of the words. The plaintiff should have considered the possibility of this happening before he assented to publication.

In *Cookson v Harewood* (1932), the plaintiff sued the defendants for libel because they had published a true statement that the plaintiff had been warned off all pony racing tracks under their control. The plaintiff had submitted to the rules of the Pony Turf Club which the defendants controlled and one of these rules was that the stewards of the club might, in their absolute discretion, warn off any person. The plaintiff contended that if, by innuendo, the jury interpreted the statement as meaning that he had been guilty of corrupt and fraudulent practices, then the defendants were liable. The Court of Appeal held that this argument was unsound. Scrutton LJ maintained there was no liability if it was a true statement and there was authority to publish the true statement, it did not matter what people understood it to mean. In the same way, if a statement is defamatory its meaning does not matter, it is still defamatory.

Defences

Offer to make amends

A defence of offer of amends is contained in ss 2–4 of the Defamation Act 1996. This repeals the previous defence of unintentional defamation contained in s 4 of the Defamation Act 1952.

A person who has published a statement alleged to be defamatory of another may make an offer of amends.

The offer may be in relation to the statement generally or in relation to a specific defamatory meaning which the person making the offer accepts that the statement conveys ('a qualified offer'). A qualified offer would be made where a defendant accepts that the statement is partially untrue or where the defendant claims the statement is intended to have a less serious meaning than that claimed by a plaintiff. For example, a newspaper runs a story about a surgeon who is involved in an operation that has had a disastrous outcome. The surgeon claims that the article is imputing malice but the newspaper claims that it is an allegation of incompetence. The newspaper could make a qualified offer in relation to the less serious meaning. If the offer is refused, the newspaper would have a defence, if it was found that the statement meant incompetence.

An offer to make amends must comply with the following criteria, under s 3 of the Defamation Act 1996:

- it must be in writing;
- must be expressed to be an offer to make amends under s 2 of the Defamation Act 1996;
- must state whether it is a qualified offer and, if so, set out the defamatory meaning in relation to what is made.

An offer to make amends is an offer to do the following:

- make a suitable correction and sufficient apology;
- to publish the correction and apology in a reasonable and practicable manner;
- to pay compensation (if any) and costs.

Where the offer is accepted, s 3 of the Defamation Act 1996 applies. Defamation proceedings cannot be brought or continued but the offer can be enforced in accordance with the section. Where the parties are agreed on the steps required to fulfil the offer, the aggrieved party may apply to the court for an order that the party take the agreed steps. If the parties do not agree on the correction, apology and publication, the party who made the offer may make the correction and apology in open court in terms approved by the court, and give an undertaking to the court as to the manner of their publication.

Where the parties do not agree, compensation and costs are determined in the same way as in defamation proceedings. Proceedings under this section are heard without a jury.

Where the offer is not accepted the situation is governed by s 4 of the Defamation Act 1996. The fact that the offer was made is a defence except where the person who made the offer knew or had reason to believe that the statement complained of referred to the plaintiff or was likely to be understood as referring to the plaintiff and was both false and defamatory. A qualified offer is only a defence in respect of the meaning to which the offer related. The offer can also be relied on in mitigation of damages, whether or not it was used as a defence.

The new offer to make amends defence differs from the previous defence of unintentional defamation, in that the defendant can be liable to pay compensation, even in cases of unintentional defamation. Under the old defence, only an apology and costs would have been paid.

Justification

Justification consists of proof that the allegedly defamatory matter was true. Justification is a dangerous defence because, if it fails, heavier damages will be awarded. On the other hand, if the defendant's statement are true, the defence will avail even if he did not believe them to be true or made them with malice.

Onus of proof

The defendant must prove that the statement was true as opposed to the plaintiff proving its falsity. Justification must be specially pleaded.

Substantial truth suffices

It is sufficient to prove the substantial truth of the statement, ie a minor inaccuracy will not vitiate the defence. Whether the inaccuracy was minor is a matter of fact for the jury.

In *Alexander v North Eastern Railway Company* (1865), a sentence of 'five or fourteen days' was reported as 'five or three weeks'. This was held to be not sufficiently inaccurate to defeat justification. Conversely, however, 'the justification must be as broad as the charge'.

In *Lewis v Daily Telegraph* (1964), the defendants printed an article stating that the fraud squad were inquiring into the affairs of the plaintiff company. It was alleged that the words were defamatory on their 'ordinary and literal meaning'. The defendants were able to justify the words according to their ordinary and literal meaning. The House of Lords held that the words were incapable of being defamatory *per se*. Therefore, the defence of justification is distinct from the question whether the words are defamatory; although the two are interlocked to some extent.

Effect of the Defamation Act 1952

Section 5 provides that justification will not fail merely because the truth of one of several charges is not established, if, having regard to the other charges, it did not do material injury to the plaintiff's reputation.

Problems in the working of s 5 in practice were revealed by *Speidel v Plato Films* (1961). The plaintiff was the subject of a film made by the defendants, in which several allegations were made against him. The plaintiff only complained about two specific allegations, which the defendant was unable to prove, although they were able to prove equally discreditable allegations. The wider content of the film could not be introduced by the defendants to prove that the overall effect of the film had not damaged the plaintiff's reputation and because only specific allegations had been complained of s 5 did not come into effect. It was possible, however, to prove that the plaintiff had a bad reputation in order to reduce the amount of damages.

The rule in *Plato v Speidel Films* (1961) only applies where there are distinct allegations and will not apply where allegations have a common sting. In *Polly Peck (Holdings) plc v Trelford* (1986), the plaintiff claimed damages in respect of the whole of one article and parts of two others. The defendant pleaded justification and fair comment. It was held that the defendant could prove the truth of the sting by proving the truth of the statements which the plaintiff has not complained of.

The Faulks committee recommended the amendment of s 5 so that the defendant could rely on the whole publication in assessing the truth of a selected part.

Defendant's motive irrelevant

The defence of justification, if otherwise good, will not fail because the defendant acted from a malicious or improper motive. However, an honest and reasonable but mistaken belief in the statement will not suffice to support justification.

Rehabilitation of Offenders Act 1974

Section 8 provides that where the plaintiff was defamed by the raising against him of a 'spent' conviction, proof of the truth of the allegation will not avail as a defence if the statement was published with malice.

In the past, the application of the principles concerning the defence of justification gave rise to particular difficulty where the defamatory statement was to the effect that the plaintiff had been convicted of a criminal offence. At common law a conviction was not even *prima facie* evidence of guilt for the purposes of other proceedings and this meant that the defendant had to prove the guilt for the purposes of other proceedings which in turn meant that the defendant had to prove the guilt of the plaintiff again if the defence of justification was to succeed.

However, by s 13 of the Civil Evidence Act 1968, in an action for libel or slander, where the question is whether a person committed a criminal offence, the fact that he stands convicted of the offence is conclusive evidence that he did commit it.

Rumour

It was held in *Aspro Travel Ltd v Owners Abroad Group plc* (1995) that hearsay and rumour could not constitute justification for an assertion of fact in defamation proceedings. However, in certain circumstances a person could repeat a rumour before being satisfied that it is true and plead in justification that there are such rumours.

Fair comment on a matter of public interest

Definition

Fair comment is comment honestly made on a matter of public interest.

Comment means opinion

The defendant must prove that the statement was comment, ie one of opinion, not fact. If the statement consists of facts, justification is the appropriate defence.

In *London Artists Ltd v Littler* (1969) the defendant, a well-known impresario, was presenting a play in the West End. Four of the leading actors, through their agent, London Artists Ltd, simultaneously gave notice to leave the cast. The defendant in a letter published in the press, alleged a conspiracy by them to being the run of the play to an end. When sued for libel, he raised a defence of fair comment. The defence failed, the allegation of conspiracy was, in the circumstances, a statement of fact, not of opinion and therefore not 'comment'. Whereas, in

Dakhyl v Labouchere (1908), the plaintiff described himself as a 'special-ist for the treatment of deafness, ear, nose and throat diseases'. The defendant described him as 'a quack of the rankest species'. The House of Lords held that this might be comment.

Good faith is essential
The defendant must have made the comment in good faith, ie believ-ing in the truth of the statement and without malicious distortion. In *Telnikoff v Matusevitch* (1990), it was held by the Court of Appeal that the comment need only be considered fair by an objective test, ie would a reasonable man have an held an honest belief in the truth of the statement. This is a question of burden of proof. The defendant does not have to prove that he had an honest belief in the truth of the statement, it is for the plaintiff to prove that the defendant acted with malice.

A newspaper publishing a letter does not lose the defence of fair comment simply because it cannot prove that its' correspondent did not have an honest belief in the statement (*Lyon v Daily Telegraph* (1943)).

Public interest is essential
The defendant must prove that the matter commented on was one of public interest. This is given a wide definition. Lord Denning in *London Artists v Littler* (1969) said:

> Whenever a matter is such as to affect people at large, so that they may be legitimately interested in, or concerned at, what is going on; or what may happen to them or to others; then it is a matter of pub-lic interest on which everyone is entitled to make a fair comment.

Fairness is not synonymous with moderation
Although the comment must be fair, ie the honestly held opinion of the defendant, 'fair comment does not mean moderate comment'. The opinion of the court or the jury must not be substituted for that of the defendant (*McQuire v Western Morning News* (1903)). The test is 'Was this an opinion, however exaggerated, obstinate or prejudiced, which was honestly held by the writer?' (*Silkin v Beaverbrook Newspapers Ltd* (1958)) *per* Diplock J. This lead the Faulks committee to recommend that 'fair comment' should be changed to 'comment'.

Fact and comment
Section 6 of the Defamation Act 1952 provides that in an action for libel and slander in respect of words consisting partly of allegations of fact

and partly expressions of opinion, a defence of fair comment shall not fail by reason only that the truth of every allegation of fact is not proved, if the expression of opinion is fair comment having regard to such of the facts alleged or referred to in the words complained of as are proved. Formerly, the slightest inaccuracy in the facts stated defeated fair comment.

The 'rolled up' plea

Fact and comment are difficult to separate. Because of this the plea is sometimes couched in the terms 'in so far as the words complained of are statements of fact they are true in substance and in fact; and in so far as they consist of comment they are fair comment on a matter of public interest'. This is the 'rolled up' plea – a plea of fair comment, not justification. The facts are proved merely to lay a foundation for the defence of fair comment. Furthermore, the Rules of Court provide that the plaintiff is entitled to be informed of the facts on which the defendant intends to rely.

It is not necessary to set out all the facts on which the writer has based his opinion. A passing reference to the facts can be sufficient, as in *Kemsley v Foot* (1952). The defendant attacked an article in the Evening Standard. The article appeared under the heading 'Lower than Kemsley' but no other reference was made to Kemsley, who was a newspaper proprietor. This was a sufficient reference to the facts on which the opinion had been based, ie the conduct of the Kemsley press.

It is not possible when determining whether the comment is fact or opinion to have regard to other documents incorporated into the statement. In *Telnikoff v Matusevitch* (1991), the defendant had published a letter in a newspaper in response to an article published by the plaintiff, which was referred to in the letter. The House of Lords held that it was not possible to look at the article in determining whether the letter was a statement of fact or opinion.

Where the defendant's comments are based on a report of judicial proceedings, the onus is on the defendant to prove that the report is fair and accurate and therefore privileged. In *Brent Walker plc v Time Out Ltd* (1991), the defendant pleaded fair comment based on privileged statements made about the plaintiff at a trial in 1956. The plaintiff claimed that the statements did not form part of a fair and accurate report of the proceedings. It was held that the defendant had to show that the report was fair and accurate.

Malice

Malice may defeat fair comment. The malice must distort the comment to vitiate the defence. In *Thomas v Bradbury Agnew & Co Ltd* (1906) the writer of a review made untrue allegations of fact and harboured personal spite against the author. The comment was distorted by malice and therefore not fair.

Absolute privilege

A statement which is absolutely privileged is not actionable under any circumstances. The following classes of statements are absolutely privileged:

Those made in either House of Parliament

This stems from the Bill of Rights 1689, which stated: 'The freedom of speech and debates of the proceedings of Parliament ought not to be impeached or questioned in any court or place outside of Parliament.'

The Privy Council case of *Prebble v Television New Zealand Ltd* (1994) held that parliamentary privilege prohibits any suggestion being made in court proceedings that statements made in the House were lies or motivated by a desire to mislead and also prohibits suggestions that legislation was passed as part of a conspiracy. It was also held that an individual Member of Parliament could not override parliamentary privilege, as privilege belonged to Parliament itself.

It was held in *Allason v Haines* (1995) that it would be a breach of parliamentary privilege to bring evidence of a Member of Parliament's behaviour in the House of Commons. However, the action was stayed, as this deprived the defendants' of their defence.

The common law position has now been changed as a result of s 13 of the Defamation Act 1996. This allows a person, where his conduct in or in relation to proceedings in Parliament is in issue in defamation proceedings, to waive, so far as concerns him, the protection of any enactment or rule of law which prevents proceedings in Parliament being impeached or questioned in any court or place outside Parliament. This enables a Member of either House of Parliament to clear his name if he is alleged to have acted dishonestly or improperly in connection with his parliamentary duties.

Reports of Parliamentary proceedings

Reports of Parliamentary Proceedings published by order of either House, or their re-publication in full (Parliamentary Papers Act 1840).

Judicial proceedings

Statements made by judges, advocates, witnesses or parties:

- in the course of judicial proceedings, civil or military; or
- with reference to such proceedings.

Addis v Crocker (1961) extended this immunity to tribunals exercising judicial as distinct from administrative functions. An order of the Disciplinary Tribunal of the Law Society was therefore held to be absolutely privileged.

A licensing application is an administrative function and is not privileged (*Royal Aquarium Society Ltd v Parkinson* (1892)).

Communications between lawyer and client

Professional communications between solicitor and client possess qualified privilege on the grounds that the interests of justice demand it. The communication must be made by or to the solicitor in his professional capacity and must be relevant to the relationship of solicitor and client, having regard to the business in hand.

It seems generally agreed that the privilege is qualified but the point is not absolutely free from doubt since the Court of Appeal has treated it on separate occasions as both absolute and qualified and in *Minter v Priest* (1930) the House of Lords expressly reserved its opinion.

Officers of State

A statement is absolutely privileged if made by one officer of state to another in the course of official duty. *Chatterton v Secretary of State for India* (1895) involved a communication by a Minister to the Under Secretary of State for India to enable him to answer a parliamentary question. That was privileged.

The following have been held to be 'officers of state':

- a military officer reporting to his superiors;
- a Minister communicating with an official;
- a High Commissioner reporting to Prime Minister.

Statements made in the UK by officials of foreign governments are probably protected by diplomatic immunity.

Husband and wife

Statements made by one spouse to another are absolutely privileged but statements by one spouse to a third party about the other are not.

Reports of court proceedings

Under s 14 of the Defamation Act 1996, a fair and accurate report of proceedings before a court is absolutely privileged if published contemporaneously with proceedings. Where reports of proceedings are postponed by court order or statutory provision, a publication is treated as contemporaneous if it as published as soon as is practicable after permission is granted. The section applies to:

- any court in the United Kingdom;
- the European Court of Justice and any court attached to that court;
- the European Court of Human Rights;
- any international criminal tribunal established by the Security Council of the United Nations or by an international agreement to which the United Kingdom is a party.

Qualified privilege

For a statement to enjoy qualified privilege there must be:

- a legal, moral or social duty to make it on one side;
- a corresponding interest to receive it on the other.

Both these conditions must be satisfied.

Reports of parliamentary, judicial and public proceedings

Reports of the statements should not be confused with the statements themselves, eg by a judge in court or an MP in the House, which are absolutely privileged.

Fair and accurate reports of judicial proceedings

Public proceedings in any court of justice enjoy qualified privilege at common law. This extends to foreign courts if the matter is of legitimate interest to the British public.

This privilege does not extend to:

- tribunals to which the public is not admitted;
- domestic tribunals;
- cases of which the subject matter is obscene or blasphemous.

Fair and accurate reports of parliamentary debates

This extends to certain other bodies, such as statutory commissions, where it is in the public interest that their proceedings should be published.

Section 15 Defamation Act 1996

Section 15 gives qualified privilege to the publication of any report or statement of certain reports and statements.

The section only applies to publication of documents which are of public concern and public benefit.

In some cases, the defence of qualified privilege cannot be raised if the defendant failed to accede 'in a suitable manner' to a request by the plaintiff to publish a reasonable letter or statement by way of explanation or contradiction.

Statements which do not require explanation or contradiction

Fair and accurate reports of proceedings of legislatures, courts, public inquiries and international organisations anywhere in the world. Fair and accurate copies of public documents, court notices and documents of legislatures, governments and international organisations which have been published anywhere in the world.

Statements which do require explanation or contradiction

This includes, *inter alia*, fair and accurate reports of public meetings, general meetings of a UK public company and certain associations. Fair and accurate reports of notices issued for the information of the public of legislatures, governments or governmental authorities of Member States, the European Parliament, the European Commission, international organisations and conferences and documents of any court of any Member State or the European Court of Justice, made available by a judge or officer of the court.

Duty and interest

Statements made by A to B about C where A has a legal, moral or social duty to communicate to B and which B has a corresponding interest in receiving or where A has an interest to be protected and B is under a corresponding legal, moral or social duty to protect that interest.

The case of *Watt v Longsdon* (1930) establishes that the reciprocal duty and interest are essential in all cases of qualified privilege, not only those in which the allegedly defamatory statement was made in discharge of a duty. In this case, the plaintiff and defendant were members of the same firm. Another member of the firm wrote to the defendant, making defamatory statements about the plaintiff's morals and behaviour. The defendant showed the letter to the chairman of the firm and to the plaintiff's wife. It was held that publication to the chairman was privileged, since there was a reciprocal duty to make it and a reciprocal duty to receive it; but publication to the plaintiff's wife was not privileged; she had an interest to receive the statement but the defendant had no duty to show her the letter.

In *Beach v Freeson* (1971), a letter by a Member of Parliament to the Law Society and the Lord Chancellor in which he set out complaints from one of his constituents concerning the conduct of a firm of solicitors was held to be protected by qualified privilege.

So, complaints about the conduct of public authorities or of those with responsibilities to the public are generally protected by qualified privilege provided they are made in good faith and communicated to a person with the proper interest in the subject matter.

Statements made in protection of oneself or one's property

In *Osborn v Boulter* (1930), a publican complained to the brewers who supplied him with beer that it was of poor quality. They retorted that they had heard rumours that the poor quality of the beer was due to the watering of it by the publican and they published this statement to a third party. It was held to be privileged.

Malice

A plea of unqualified privilege can be rebutted by proof of express malice and malice in this connection may mean either:

- lack of belief in the truth of the statement;
- use of the privileged occasion for an improper purpose.

Horrocks v Lowe (1974) held that mere carelessness or even honest belief produced by irrational prejudice, does not amount to malice.

The malice of an agent may make the innocent principal liable in some cases on the ordinary principles of vicarious liability but the malice of the principal cannot do the same for the innocent agent (*Egger v Viscount Chelmsford* (1964)).

Remedies

Injunction

Where there is an imminent threat to someone's reputation an injunction may be obtained in order to prevent the publication of defamatory material.

Damages

Nominal damages

These are awarded where the case has been proved but the plaintiff has suffered very little damage.

Contemptuous damages

These are awarded where the plaintiff has been technically successful but the claim is without merit, eg *Plato v Speidel Films* (1961).

Exemplary damages

These can be awarded where the defendant has calculated that even after paying out damages and costs he will still make a profit if he commits the tort, eg by defaming someone but making a profit through increased circulation of his newspaper (*Cassell & Co v Broome* (1972)).

Excessive damages

The level of damages in defamation cases are set by juries who seem to set the awards at a disproportionately high level, particularly in comparison to personal injury cases. Until recently, the Court of Appeal could not reduce high awards of damages in libel cases unless the jury had been misdirected. The situation changed with the introduction of s 8 of the Courts and Legal Services Act 1990. The Court of Appeal can now substitute a fresh award if the original award is 'excessive or inadequate'.

In *Sutcliffe v Pressdram Ltd* (1990), the plaintiff who is the wife of a serial killer was awarded £600,000 damages by a jury after Private Eye alleged that she had sold her story. On appeal, damages were reduced as they wrongly contained an element of exemplary damages.

A new approach was used in *Rantzen v Mirror Group Newspapers* (1993) by using a combination of s 8 of the Courts and Legal Services Act 1990 and Article 10 of the European Convention on Human Rights. The plaintiff had been awarded £250,000 in damages. The defendants claimed that the size of the award inhibited their right to free speech. The Court of Appeal said that 'excessive' damages had to be interpreted in the light of Article 10 which only allows those restrictions on free speech which are 'necessary'. The Convention was said to underlie common law principles relating to free speech. The damages awarded should be proportionate to the damage suffered and were therefore reduced to £110,000.

The European Court of Human Rights ruled that libel damages of £1.5 million were a violation of Article 10 of the European Convention on Human Rights in *Tolstoy Miloslavsky v United Kingdom* (1995). It was found that judicial control at the trial and on appeal, did not offer adequate and effective safeguards against a disproportionately large award. At the relevant time, an award could only be overturned if it was so unreasonable that it could only be arrived at capriciously, unconscionably or irrationally. The combination of the Courts and

Legal Services Act 1990 and principles of free expression now mean that awards can be overturned on appeal, on the grounds that they are excessive.

Judicial control over the awards made by juries has been further strengthened by the Defamation Act 1996 (see below) and the case of *John v MGN Ltd* (1995), as judges can now give guidance as to the amount of compensation. Sir Thomas Bingham MR (as he then was) also said in that case that although Article 10 of the European Convention on Human Rights was not part of English law there was no conflict or discrepancy between that and the common law.

The new guidelines were used in *Kiam v Neill* (1996). In that case, an award of £45,000 to a businessman who had allegations of defaulting on a loan and insolvency made against him was not excessive. The Court of Appeal held that the jury could take into account the prominence of the plaintiff's reputation, the fact that it struck at the core of his life's achievement and that it had a prolonged and significant effect on him personally. The extent of publication is also relevant.

The Defamation Act 1996 aims to create a new fast track for libel cases, by having smaller cases handled summarily by judges alone. Plaintiffs are able to go straight to a judge for a correction. Damages of up to £10,000 can be awarded.

There are new defences of offers of amends to defendants that did not intend to defame and are willing to pay damages assessed by a judge and to publish an appropriate correction and apology.

Fast track procedure

Sections 8–10 of the Defamation Act 1996 introduce new powers for the court to dispose summarily of the plaintiff's claim. The purpose of the procedure is to simplify, expedite and reduce the costs of the simpler defamation claims.

Section 8 gives the judge the power to dismiss the case summarily. The claim can be dismissed if it has no realistic prospect of success and there is no reason why it should be tried. The plaintiff can be given judgment and summary relief if there is no defence with a reasonable prospect of success and there is no reason why it should be tried. Section 9 sets out summary relief, as follows:

- a declaration that the statement was false and defamatory;
- an order that the defendant publish a suitable correction and apology;
- damages not exceeding £10,000; an order restraining the defendant from publishing or further publishing the matter complained of.

The content of any correction and apology, and the manner of publication is for the parties to agree but in the absence of agreement the court may give directions. This has led to criticisms that the procedure enters into the area of editorial responsibility.

Doubt has been cast on whether the fast track procedure can fulfil its aims of expediting and simplifying procedure. It potentially adds a new stage to every defamation trial, there is little guidance as to how judges are to decide cases under this procedure and there will still be areas of conflict between the parties, such as the suitability of the procedure to the case in question and points of evidence. Legal aid is not available for the procedure, although the Lord Chancellor has said that he is considering it.

8 General defences

So far, we have been primarily concerned with what a plaintiff has to prove in order to establish the existence of a tort. This would be a convenient point to consider certain defences which may be raised by the defendant, who while admitting the behaviour complained of (which would otherwise constitute a tort), then seeks to adduce in evidence additional facts which will excuse what he has done. So, the burden of proving the facts to establish the defence rests on the defendant.

Contributory negligence

Position at common law

At common law, it was a complete defence if the defendant proved that the plaintiff had been guilty of contributory negligence. In *Butterfield v Forrester* (1809), the defendant negligently left a pole lying across the road. The plaintiff was injured when he collided with the pole when riding along the road. Although the defendant had been negligent he escaped liability since the plaintiff would have avoided the accident if he had not been riding so fast.

Last opportunity
This resulted in undue hardship to the plaintiff and so to mitigate its harshness the courts developed the rule of 'last opportunity' which meant that whoever was negligent last in time was treated as the sole

cause of the damage on the basis that they had been the last one to have the opportunity to avoid the accident. The rule was applied in *Davies v Mann* (1842). The plaintiff tied the feet of his donkey and negligently left him on the highway. The defendant who was driving his wagon faster than necessary collided with, and killed, the donkey. The defendant was liable. If he had been driving at the correct speed, he would have avoided the donkey, so he had the last opportunity to avoid the accident.

Furthermore, if but for the defendant's negligence he would have had the last opportunity he was again treated as if he had the last opportunity and was liable for the full loss (*British Columbia Electric Ry Co Ltd v Loach* (1916)).

Law Reform (Contributory Negligence) Act 1945

This linear sequential approach to liability was most difficult to apply in cases where events occurred simultaneously.

The problems led to the Law Reform (Contributory Negligence) Act 1945, which introduced apportionment of damages for accidents occurring on land. It is now possible for the courts to reduce the damages awarded against the defendant to the extent to which the plaintiff was contributorily negligent. It was held by the Court of Appeal in *Pitts v Hunt* (1991) that damages can never be reduced by 100% and therefore contributory negligence can only be a partial defence.

Scope of the Law Reform (Contributory Negligence) Act 1945

Under s 4 of the Act, fault means 'negligence, breach of statutory duty or other act or omission which gives rise to liability in tort'. Thus, the Act applies to nuisance and *Rylands v Fletcher* as well as negligence. There is conflicting authority as to whether the rule applies to trespass to the person, eg Salmond and Heuston believe it does not apply and Brazier in *Street on Torts* believes it does. It does not apply to trespass to goods or conversion by virtue of s 11 of the Torts (Interference with Goods) Act 1977.

In order to establish and prove contributory negligence, the defendant must plead and prove:

- that the plaintiff's injury results from the risk which the plaintiff's negligence exposed him;
- that the plaintiff's negligence contributed to his injury;
- that there was fault or negligence on the part of the plaintiff.

Plaintiff's negligence contributed to his injury

It is not necessary to show that the plaintiff owes the defendant a duty of care, merely that the plaintiff has contributed to the injury and not necessarily the cause of the accident. So, in *O'Connell v Jackson* (1972), there was a 15% reduction in the damages awarded to a motor-cyclist because of his failure to wear a crash helmet. Similarly, in *Froom v Butcher* (1975), there was a 25% reduction to a driver for failure to wear a seatbelt, as the injury could have been completely avoided by wearing the seat belt but if wearing a seat belt would have reduced the severity of the injuries then damages would have been reduced by 15%.

Other examples of the plaintiff having contributed to the injury include the failure of a motor-cyclist to fasten the chin strap of a crash helmet (*Capps v Miller* (1989)); accepting a lift in a car knowing that the driver is drunk (*Owens v Brimmell* (1977)), although the burden is on the defendant to show that the plaintiff knew that the defendant was unfit to drive (*Limbrick v French* (1993)); asking a much younger inexperienced driver to drive a car when the driver has never driven a powerful, automatic car before (*Donelan v Donelan* (1993)); crossing a pelican crossing when the pedestrian light is red (*Fitzgerald v Lane* (1989)) and injured while trespassing as a result of criminal activities (*Revill v Newberry* (1996)).

Plaintiff's injury results from the risk which he exposed himself

In *Jones v Livox Quarries Ltd* (1952), the plaintiff was riding on the back of the defendant's vehicle contrary to instructions. A vehicle collided into the back, injuring the plaintiff. He argued, unsuccessfully, that he had exposed himself to the risk of falling off, not to a collision.

The standard of care

This is the same standard of care as that in negligence *per* Lord Denning in *Jones v Livox Quarries*:

> A person is guilty of contributory negligence if he ought reasonably to have foreseen that, if he did not act as a reasonable, prudent man, he might hurt himself and in his reckoning he must take into account the possibility of others being careless.

In practice though the courts seem to demand less of plaintiffs than defendants.

Children

Denning LJ in *Gough v Thorne* (1966) said that a very young child could not be contributorily negligent. However, the general test seems to be what degree of care an infant of a particular age can reasonably be expected to take for his own safety (*Yachuk v Oliver Blais Co Ltd* (1949)). Consequently, a 12-year-old girl was contributorily negligent in *Armstrong v Cotterell* (1993), as a child of that age is expected to know the basic elements of the Highway Code.

It was held in *Oliver v Birmingham and Midland Omnibus Co Ltd* (1933) that where a child is under the control of an adult, negligence on the part of the adult is not imputed to the child.

Accidents at work

The purpose of such statutory regulations as the Factories Acts is to ensure the safety standards in workplaces and to protect workers from their own carelessness.

This being the purpose behind such regulations in order to ensure that their purpose is not defeated by finding contributory negligence, the courts tend to be less willing to make a finding of contributory negligence in these cases (see *Caswell v Powell Duffryn Associated Colleries Ltd* (1940)).

This does not mean that a workman can never be guilty of contributory negligence. In *Jayes v IMI (Kynoch)Ltd* (1985) a workman who put his hand into a piece of moving machinery had his damages reduced by 100%, even though the employer was in breach of his statutory duty to fence the machinery. It should be noted that this case was heard prior to *Pitts v Hunt* (1990) and damages can now never be reduced by 100%.

Emergency

An emergency is a special situation in which a person's reactions may, with hindsight, be regarded as negligent. The law takes account of this and provided the plaintiff has acted reasonably he will not be held to have been contributorily negligent (see *Jones v Boyce* (1816)).

Consent/*volenti non fit injuria*

There is considerable confusion between these two concepts. Consent is used to describe the defence that may be used when sued for committing an intentional tort.

Volenti non fit injuria is the appropriate term where the plaintiff alleges negligence/strict liability tort, ie an unintentional tort, which claims the defendant's voluntary assumption of the risk involved. However, the general principles applying to both concepts are the same but it is important to bear in mind the stature of the tort concerned.

The defence of consent was found to be available to a defendant who clamped the plaintiff's car in *Arthur v Anker* (1995). However, certain conditions had to be satisfied before the defence would arise. There would have to be a notice that a vehicle parked without lawful authority would be clamped and released on payment of a fee. The release fee would have to be reasonable. The vehicle would have to be released without delay, once the owner had offered to pay and there would have to be means by which the owner could communicate his offer of payment.

Mere knowledge does not imply consent

In the case of *Smith v Baker and Sons* (1891), the plaintiff was an employee of the defendants and was employed in drilling holes and rock cutting and was aware of the danger of a crane continually swinging over his head. A stone fell out of the crane and injured him. He brought an action in negligence and *volenti non fit injuria* was pleaded.

It was held that mere knowledge of the risk was not enough; it had to be shown that the plaintiff had consented to the particular thing being done which would involve the risk and consented to take that risk upon himself.

The question in *Dann v Hamilton* (1939) was whether a plaintiff who accepted a lift from a drunk driver who was obviously inebriated could be taken to have assumed the risk of injury. It was held that *volenti* did not apply, unless the drunkenness was so extreme and so glaring that accepting lift was equivalent to 'walking on the edge of an unfenced cliff'.

Under s 149 of the Road Traffic Act 1988 defendants are prevented from relying on the *volenti* defence where a passenger sues a driver in circumstances where, under the Act, insurance is compulsory. It does not apply where there is no requirement of compulsory insurance under the Act, for example, an aeroplane. In *Morris v Murray* (1990), two men involved in a drinking session took a plane on a flight. The plane crashed but the plaintiff passenger was held to be *volens* as he must have known the state the pilot was in.

To be effective consent must be freely given

Normally, as already shown by in *Smith v Baker and Sons*, an employee will rarely be held to be *volens* but there are exceptional cases such as *ICI v Shatwell* (1965). The plaintiff and his brother disregarded the instructions of their employer and were also in breach of statutory safety regulations and chose to test certain detonators without seeking the necessary precautions. The plaintiff was injured in the subsequent explosion. The plaintiff's action in both negligence and breach of statutory duty failed because of *volenti non fit injuria*. This is an unusual case, however, and *volens* will not normally arise out of an employee's ordinary duties.

Rescue cases

The law is reluctant to apply *volenti* to rescue situations, because to do so would negative the duty of care owed to the plaintiff.

In *Haynes v Harwood* (1935), a two horse van was left unattended in the street. A boy threw a stone, the horses ran off and threatened a woman and children. A policeman intercepted and stopped the horses but was injured. It was held that the *volenti* defence did not apply. *Volenti* will apply where there is no real risk of danger and there is not a genuine emergency (*Cutler v United Dairies (London) Ltd* (1933)).

Illegal acts

A person who is engaged in an illegal act at the time he is injured may be precluded from a civil claim by the maxim *ex turpi causa non oritur actio* (bad people get less).

A distinction was made by Asquith LJ in *National Coal Board v England* between two different types of situation:

- the case of two burglars on their way to commit a burglary and while proceeding one picks the other's pocket; and
- where they have agreed to open a safe by means of high explosive and one negligently handles the explosive charge injuring the other.

In the first situation, he thought that there would be liability in tort but not in the second. The idea being that where the illegality is incidental to the cause of action in tort then recovery in tort may still be allowed.

It was held in *Ashton v Turner* (1980) that one participant in a burglary could not succeed against his fellow participant who crashed the car while driving away at high speed from the scene of the crime.

In the case of *Pitts v Hunt* (1990), the plaintiff was a pillion passenger on a motorcycle. Both the plaintiff and the defendant who was riding the motorcycle were drunk. The plaintiff also knew that the defendant was unlicensed and uninsured. The defendant carelessly crashed the motorcycle, killing himself and injuring the plaintiff. Due to s 149 of the Road Traffic Act 1988, the defence of *volenti* did not apply. Nevertheless, the plaintiff was found to be *ex turpi*. The majority of the Court of Appeal held that because of the joint illegal activity it was impossible to determine the standard of care.

Most cases have not followed this standard of care test but have instead used a test based on whether it would be an affront to public conscience to compensate the plaintiff.

Recently, in the case of *Revill v Newberry* (1995), it was held that the rule did not apply in a claim for personal injuries where the plaintiff was a trespasser engaged in criminal activities and the defendant had shot the plaintiff. The defendant was found to have acted negligently and to have denied the plaintiff, who had been contributorily negligent, any compensation would have effectively made him an outlaw. The case was distinguished from a 'joint criminal enterprise' such as *Pitts v Hunt*. Evans LJ held that it is one thing to deny a plaintiff any fruits from his illegal conduct but different and more far-reaching to deprive him of compensation for injury which he had suffered and which he was otherwise entitled to recover at law.

Immoral conduct

Ex turpi applies not only to criminal conduct but can also apply to immoral conduct, as well. In *Kirkham v Chief Constable of the Greater Manchester Police* (1990), it was said that suicide committed by someone 'wholly sane' would be *ex turpi* but in that particular case it did not apply as there was grave mental instability.

Mistake

Mistake as to law or to fact, is not a general defence. Mistake is not a defence to an intentional tort such as trespass or conversion, however, reasonable.

Inevitable accident

This used to be a defence in trespass but now liability in trespass depends upon proof of intention. However, in negligence, if it can be shown that the accident could not have been avoided by the exercise of reasonable care, then that amounts to a claim that the behaviour was not negligent.

Statutory authority

A statute may authorise what would otherwise be a tort and an injured party will have no remedy save for that provided by statute. Statutes often confer powers to act on public and other authorities. Such power will not in general be a defence to a claim in tort.

Limitation of actions

In actions at common law, there is no limitation period. The rules on limitation are entirely statutory and are now contained in the Limitation Act 1980.

The basic rule is that an action cannot be brought more than six years from the date the cause of action accrued (s 2 of the Limitation Act 1980).

There are four situations in which different rules apply.

Actions for personal injury and death

In actions for personal injuries, the basic limitation period is three years from either the date on which the cause of action accrued or the date of the plaintiff's knowledge whichever is later (s 11(4) of the Limitation Act 1980). The court has a wide discretion to disregard this time limit and permit the action to proceed by virtue of s 33 of the Limitation Act 1980.

It was held by the House of Lords in *Stubbings v Webb* (1993) that s 11 of the Limitation Act 1980 only applies to personal injuries arising from negligence, nuisance or breach of a duty of care. Therefore, the limitation period for personal injuries caused by assault was six years from the date cause of action accrued.

The cause of action accrues when the plaintiff suffers actionable damage irrespective of the plaintiff's knowledge of the damage (*Cartledge v Jopling & Sons Ltd* (1963)). But the 'date of knowledge' is defined in s 15 of the Limitation Act 1980. The plaintiff has knowledge of the cause of action when he first has knowledge of the following facts:

- that the injury was significant; and
- that the injury was attributable in whole or in part to the act or omission which is alleged to constitute negligence, nuisance or breach of duty; and
- the identity of the defendant; and
- if it is alleged that the act or omission was that of a person other than the defendant, the identity of that person and the additional facts supporting the bringing of an action against the defendant.

An injury is 'significant' if it would justify proceedings against a defendant who did not dispute liability and was able to satisfy the judgment. Knowledge includes 'constructive knowledge', ie knowledge a person might reasonably have been expected to acquire.

After a major operation, the date of knowledge for the purposes of s 11 of the Limitation Act 1980 occurs as soon as the plaintiff has had time to overcome the shock of the injury, take stock of his disability and seek advice (*Forbes v Wandsworth HA* (1996)).

With regard to the discretion given by s 33, the court will have regard to all the circumstances and the exercise of the discretion is something of a lottery. The discretion was held to be unfettered in *Firman v Ellis* (1978).

By s 33(3), the court must have regard to particular aspects of the matter, eg the length and reasons for the delay; the defendant's conduct; the effect of delay on the evidence; the plaintiff's conduct, etc.

In deciding whether to exercise its discretion to disapply the three year rule under s 33 of the Limitation Act 1980, the court should apply a subjective rather than an objective test as to the reasons for the plaintiff's delay in instituting proceedings (*Coad v Cornwall and Isles of Scilly HA* (1996)).

A subjective test was again applied in *Spargo v North Essex District Health Authority* (1997).

Latent damage

Where damage is latent the plaintiff will be unaware that the damage has actually occurred. As a result, the cause of action may accrue and become statute barred before the plaintiff even knows about the damage or his right to sue.

In *Cartledge v E Jopling & Sons Ltd* (1963), the plaintiff contracted pneumoconiosis from the inhalation of dust over a long period of working in a particular environment. The damage to the lungs was latent and the plaintiff was unaware of it.

The House of Lords held that the cause of action accrued when significant damage to the lungs occurred and it was irrelevant that the plaintiff knew of the damage or not. As a result of this decision, the law of limitation was changed by statute in relation to personal injuries.

This left the problem of what to do about the defective buildings. Various tests for the commencement of the limitation period were developed. For example some felt the limitation period should begin with the date of construction; others felt that time should run when the plaintiff discovered the damage or ought reasonably to have done so.

However, the case of *Pirelli General Cable Works Ltd v Oscar Fabier & Ptnrs* (1983) held the action accrued and therefore the limitation period commenced when physical damage to the building actually occurred, regardless of whether it could be discovered by the plaintiff. A distinction is made between structural fault and the defect arising from it. The *Pirelli* case maintains that the action accrues at the time the physical damage occurs.

Pirelli has caused one or two problems. The Latent Damage Act 1986 tries to redress them. It introduced a special extension of the limitation period in respect of latent damage (other than physical injury) and it gives the plaintiff three years from the date on which he discovered significant damage. This amends the Limitation Act 1980 accordingly. All claims are subject to an absolute bar for claims for 15 years from the date of the defendant's negligence.

The Latent Damage Act 1986 is an attempt to redress the balance between the plaintiff and the defendant in latent or postponed damage cases.

The Court of Appeal in *Hallam-Eames v Merrett* (1995) held that where a plaintiff is relying on the extended limitation period provided by the Latent Damage Act 1986, he was required to have knowledge of those facts which were causally relevant for the purposes of the allegation of negligence.

Fraudulent concealment of a right of action

Where the defendant has deliberately concealed from the plaintiff the facts of a tort, the period of limitation does not commence until the plaintiff has discovered the fraud or could with reasonable diligence have done so.

Therefore, in *Kitchen v Royal Air Force Association* (1958), a failure by solicitors to inform the plaintiff of an offer of £100 by potential defendants because that might reveal their own negligence at an earlier stage, constituted deliberate concealment.

Persons under a disability

Time does not run against an infant, or a person of unsound mind, until he ceases to be under a disability or dies, whichever occurs. However, if the plaintiff was not under a disability when the action accrued but subsequently becomes of unsound mind this will not prevent time from running.

9 Remedies

You should be familiar with the following areas:

- aims of compensation
- types of damage
- structured settlements, provisional damages, interim damages
- injunctions
- death in relation to tort

In considering remedies, it should be remembered that tort compensation is not the principal form of compensation. In tort, the plaintiff's chances of receiving adequate compensation will depend on whether he can prove the defendant was at fault and whether the defendant has adequate resources to compensate the plaintiff. It should be remembered that the tort system interlinks with other compensation systems. It is no coincidence that a high proportion of tort damages are in respect of road accidents, industrial accidents and medical mishaps. The insurance system works behind the scenes to ensure that the plaintiff is adequately compensated in these types of cases. There is also an interaction between the tort system and other forms of compensation such as social security, criminal injuries compensation and workmen's compensation.

Aims of compensation

The aim of tort compensation is to restore the plaintiff to the position he would have been in had the tort not been committed (*Livingstone v Rawyards Coal Co* (1880)).

It has been argued that the compensation system is based on the wrong principles. The plaintiff is compensated for what he has actually lost. The defendant is therefore liable for a greater amount of damages if he injures a high earning plaintiff as opposed to a low earning plaintiff. It has been said that damages should be based on what the plaintiff needs rather than on what he has lost. This is particularly relevant in cases of severe injury.

Further criticisms are based on the guesswork involved in calculating future loss and that compensation depends on the fault principle. Both of these points are considered in greater depth below.

Single action and lump sum

A plaintiff can only bring one action in respect of a single wrong. He cannot maintain a second action based on the same facts merely because the damage turns out to be more extensive than was anticipated. He can recover damages once only and the cause of the action is extinguished by the action. The authority for this is *Fetter v Beale* (1699). A plaintiff failed in his claim for further damages after his medical condition deteriorated following his first award of damages.

However, if one and the same act violates two rights which are accorded separate protection by the law of torts, then there are two separate causes of action; the prosecution of one will not bar proceedings in respect of the other. So, in *Brunsden v Humphrey* (1884), a cab driven by the plaintiff collided with the defendant's van through the negligent driving of the defendant's servant. In county court proceedings, the plaintiff recovered compensation for damage to his cab. He then brought a second action in the High Court for personal injuries sustained by him in the same collision and the Court of Appeal held that this action was not barred by an earlier one.

Damages are assessed once and for all and can be awarded in the form of a lump sum or since 1989 it has been possible to receive a structured settlement, whereby the damages are divided into a lump sum and periodic payments. This principle causes difficulties where loss in the future is uncertain. In personal injury actions, the plaintiff's medical condition may become much worse or much better than expected. In the words of Lord Scarman in *Lim Poh Choo v Camden and Islington AHA* (1980):

> Knowledge of the future being denied to mankind, so much of the award as is attributed to future loss and suffering will almost surely be wrong. There is only one certainty: the future will prove the award to be either too high or too low.

Disadvantages of lump sum system

A number of criticisms have been made of the lump sum system. These can be identified, as follows:

Lump sums do not fulfil the aims of tort compensation

The aim of tort damages is to place the defendant in the position he would have been in, if the tort had not been committed. A lump sum carries with it the responsibility of investment, to ensure future income from the lump sum. If the plaintiff was to be truly compensated for his loss, then he would receive a regular income in place of his lost earnings.

Lump sums are easily dissipated

There is nothing preventing the plaintiff from spending the lump sum, before the end of the period for which it was intended that the plaintiff would be compensated for. This would leave the plaintiff making a claim against the Welfare State and be doubly compensated for a single injury.

Lump sums are expensive, delay payment and cause stress

As lump sums are a once and for all system of compensation, they tend to encourage delay prior to settlement. There is every incentive to wait until the plaintiff's condition has stabilised, as much as possible, to ensure that the *quantum* of damages reflects the plaintiff's loss as closely as possible. Because an assessment of the plaintiff's future condition involves guesswork, reliance is placed on expert reports, which frequently conflict and this increases delay and costs. There is little incentive for the defendant to settle early. The plaintiff may be in receipt of welfare payments which may pressurise him into settling early and for too little. A medical condition termed 'compensation neurosis' has been identified, whereby the plaintiff's condition fails to improve pending the outcome of the case. In addition, once the case has been settled the plaintiff has to manage a sum which is probably greater than any other he has had to deal with in his life and also ensure that it lasts for the rest of his life.

Lump sums are based on guesswork

A number of projections have to be made when assessing the plaintiff's loss under the lump sum system, eg his future condition, his future earning prospects, his promotion prospects prior to the accident, etc. A lump sum system does not allow for a change in circumstance, whereas a system of periodic payments can allow for occasional review.

Types of damage

Nominal damages

Nominal damages are awarded where the plaintiff has proved his case but has suffered no loss *(Constantine v Imperial Hotels Ltd* (1944)). The plaintiff will only be awarded a small amount of money. Nominal damage can only be awarded for those torts which are actionable *per se.*

Contemptuous damages

Contemptuous damages are awarded where the action is technically successful but is without merit and the action should not have been brought. The amount of damages is usually the smallest coin in the realm. The judge will normally order the plaintiff to pay his own costs and may even order him to pay the defendant's costs as well.

Aggravated damages

Aggravated damages are compensatory. They are awarded where the plaintiff has suffered more than can reasonably be expected in the situation. They will be awarded where the plaintiff's proper feelings of dignity and pride have been injured *(Jolliffe v Willmett & Co* (1971)). They have also been awarded where the tort was committed in a malicious, insulting or oppressive manner *(Broome v Cassell & Co Ltd* (1972)). They will not be awarded in cases of personal injury where the tort was committed in a way than was more painful than necessary as a higher award for pain and suffering will reflect this *(Kralj v McGrath* (1986); *AB v South West Water Services Ltd* (1993)).

The Law Commission in its Consultation Paper No 132 has taken the provisional view that aggravated damages should be abolished.

Exemplary damages

Exemplary damages are intended to be punitive and can therefore be distinguished from aggravated damages which are compensatory. They take the form of an additional award on top of the compensatory award. They are an exception to the rule that the aim of damages in tort is to compensate. They are unpopular with judges as they confuse the aims of the criminal and civil law and it is also thought that it is undesirable to punish a defendant without the safeguards inherent in the criminal law. By contrast, it has been argued most notably by Lord Wilberforce in *Broome v Cassell & Co Ltd* (1972) that tort has a deterrent function in addition to a compensatory function and that exemplary damages are therefore a legitimate part of the compensation system. Nevertheless, a restrictive approach has been taken and it was held in *Rookes v Barnard* (1964) that exemplary damages could only be awarded in three situations.

- Oppressive, arbitrary or unconstitutional action by servants of government. The term 'servants of the government' includes police officers and also local and central government officials. It was held in *AB v South West Water Services Ltd* (1993) that publicly owned utilities which provide a monopoly service are outside the category. A man who had been seriously assaulted by police officers was entitled to substantial exemplary damages and these damages were not reduced on the grounds of his serious previous convictions in *Treadaway v Chief Constable of West Midlands* (1994).
- Where the defendant's conduct has been calculated to make a profit for himself which exceeds the compensation payable. In *Broome v Cassell & Co Ltd* (1972), the defendants published a book which they knew contained defamatory statements about the plaintiff. They believed that the increased profits from the sale would exceed any award of damages. Compensatory damages of £15,000 were awarded and an additional £25,000 exemplary damages. In *AB v South West Water Services Ltd* (1993), it was held that covering up the existence of a tort did not come within this category.
- Where statute authorises the award of exemplary damages.

In *AB v South West Water Services Ltd* (1993), it was held by the Court of Appeal that exemplary damages could not be awarded in negligence, deceit, breach of statutory duty or public nuisance. This reasoning was based on *Rookes v Barnard* (1964). The House of Lords had attempted to limit exemplary damages in that case and therefore it is not possible to award such damages unless they were available for that type of tort prior to 1964. The Law Commission is currently looking at exemplary damages and its review includes looking at this restriction.

Their provisional view is that exemplary damages should be retained but on a principled basis. However, reform would depend on the principle adopted. If the basis was that deterrence was a legitimate function of the law of tort it could extend to all torts committed deliberately, maliciously or possible recklessly. If, on the other hand, exemplary damages were based on the need for the law to protect certain interests, eg in housing, discrimination and police malpractice cases it would be confined to a narrower range of torts. It also favours codification of the law.

General and special damages

There are two meanings to these terms. First, general damages can mean the damage that is presumed to flow from torts which are actionable *per se*, eg trespass and special damage is the damage the plaintiff must prove where damage is an element of the tort, eg negligence.

The second and most common meaning is that general damages are those which cannot be calculated precisely, whereas special damages are those which can be calculated precisely at the date of trial.

Damages in personal injury actions

A plaintiff who suffers injuries incurs two types of loss. Pecuniary loss, eg loss of earnings, expenses, etc and non-pecuniary loss, eg pain and suffering, loss of a limb. The main heads of damage are:

Medical and other expenses

Under s 2(4) of the Law Reform (Personal Injuries) Act 1948, the plaintiff may incur private medical expenses and recover the same, despite the availability of the NHS. The Pearson Commission recommended that private medical expenses should only be recoverable where it was reasonable that they should be incurred on medical grounds but this proposal has not been implemented.

Section 5 of the Administration of Justice Act 1982 provides that where an injured person makes a saving by being maintained at public expense in a hospital, nursing home or other institution, then these savings must be set off against his loss of income.

If the plaintiff has to change to special accommodation as a result of his injuries, then the additional annual cost over ordinary accommodation is recoverable. The cost of adapting accommodation or a car to special needs is also recoverable. The capital cost of special accommodation or car is not recoverable as it is an asset which belongs to the plaintiff.

An example of an additional expense incurred as a result of a tort is contained in *Jones v Jones* (1984). The plaintiff's injuries led to the breakdown of his marriage. The Court of Appeal held that the extra cost to the plaintiff of having to finance two homes instead of one was, in principle, recoverable. This case has been criticised on the basis that it is not felt that marriage breakdown is really foreseeable. By contrast, it was held in *Pritchard v JH Cobden Ltd* (1987) that the cost of a marriage breakdown caused by injuries were not recoverable either because it was too remote or on grounds that it was contrary to public policy.

In *Donnelly v Joyce* (1974), the plaintiff's loss included the cost incurred by a third party. For example, where a relative or friend provides nursing assistance or financial assistance, then this can be catered for in the plaintiff's claim. Where a relative has given up work, then the loss of earnings will be recoverable provided they do not exceed the commercial cost of nursing care (*Housecroft v Burnett* (1986)).

Recently, the Law Commission has proposed in its Consultation Paper 144 that the National Health Service (NHS) should recover its costs where a patient has suffered personal injuries and someone else has been held negligent as a result of the accident.

This would bring the NHS into line with private medicine where medical costs can already be recouped. However, the effect of the change would be to increase motor insurance premiums. Motoring requires compulsory insurance. In a motor accident, the plaintiff knows that the defendant will be solvent because of the existence of insurance and therefore worth suing. It means that ultimately all motorists will bear the cost of motoring accidents and not just those at fault. Recouping the money will also involve very high administrative costs.

Loss of earnings

This can be divided into actual loss and future loss.

Actual loss runs from the date of the accident to the date of assessment (settlement or trial). It is not permissible to profit from loss of earnings, so income tax and social security contributions must be deducted in order to ascertain the net loss (*BTC v Gourley* (1956)). Loss of perquisites, for example, a company car are also taken into account.

Future loss is speculative and relates to losses the plaintiff will suffer after the date of assessment.

Section 10 of the Civil Evidence Act 1995 allows actuarial tables to be admissible in evidence to 'assess general damages for future pecuniary loss'. Although this is designed to reduce some of the problems associated with guesswork, it should be remembered that actuarial tables are compiled with life insurance and not compensation in mind.

First, it is necessary to calculate the net loss of earnings, this is known as the multiplicand. Tax and social security contributions are deducted from the plaintiff's earnings to arrive at the net figure. The mulitplicand is adjusted to take account of future promotion prospects.

The mulitplicand is multiplied by an appropriate multiplier up to a maximum of 18. In practice, the multiplier is rarely this high as it is discounted to take account of future uncertainties and also accelerated receipt. A return on capital invested is taken as 4.5% and the sum awarded which is invested should provide for lost earnings, the plaintiff being expected to live off the investment income and part of the capital. Future inflation is not taken into account as that should be covered by shrewd investment. In cases of very large awards, the House of Lords held in *Hodgson v Trapp* (1988) that the multiplier could not be increased to reflect the fact that the plaintiff would be paying tax at higher tax levels.

There has been a flurry of recent case law concerning the multiplier. At first instance, in *Wells v Wells* (1995); *Thomas v Brighton Health Authority* (1995) and *Page v Sheerness Steel Co plc* (1995), the judge fixed the multiplier by reference to the return on index-linked government securities at 3% a year. These are safe investments, involving minimum risk. The effect was to make the multiplier significantly higher and the damages were greatly increased. All three cases were heard together in the Court of Appeal in 1996 where it was held that the assumption in large awards was that the plaintiff would seek advice on how to manage the money. A basket of investment would include a substantial proportion of riskier equities as well as index-linked government securities. Consequently, the conventional discount rate of 4.5% continued to apply.

'Lost years'

Where the plaintiff's life expectancy has been reduced as a result of his injuries, the question is whether the plaintiff can be compensated for the earnings he would have received between the date of his expected death and date he would have stopped working if it had not have been for the accident. It was held in *Oliver v Ashman* (1962) that claims for the lost years were not recoverable.

The House of Lords overruled *Oliver v Ashman* in *Pickett v British Rail Engineering* (1980) and damages for prospective loss of earnings are now awarded for the whole of the plaintiff's pre-accident life expectancy, subject to deduction of the plaintiff's living expenses.

In *Phipps v Brooks Dry Cleaning Services Ltd* (1996), it was held that an award of damages for loss of earnings in the lost years was subject to a deduction for living expenses of the injured person and his dependants. This brings the position into line with that in fatal accident claims.

Social security and private insurance payments

Some social security payments are deducted in full from the plaintiff's loss of income, others are deducted at half the value of any payments. Section 22 of the Social Security Act 1989 which is now incorporated into the Social Security Administration Act 1992 enables welfare payments made to the plaintiff to be recouped from the defendant. The scheme applies to any compensation payment made after 3 September 1990 in respect of an accident or injury occurring on or after 1 January 1989 or in the case of diseases, where the first claim for benefit was made after that date.

The amount of any relevant benefit paid or to be paid in the future to the plaintiff must be disregarded when assessing damages in respect of any accident, injury or disease. The defendant deducts from the damages that he pays to the plaintiff the sum equal to the gross amount of the benefit paid or likely to be paid to the plaintiff during the relevant period and pays it instead to the Secretary of State. The defendant first notifies the amount to be deducted and then makes the deduction notifying the plaintiff of the details.

The relevant period is five years from the date of the accident, injury or first claim for the disease but a payment in final discharge of the plaintiff's claim before the end of five years will bring the the 'relevant period' to an end.

Relevant benefits are: attendance allowance, disablement benefit or pension, family credit, income support, invalidity pension and allowance, benefits payable under the Industrial Injuries and Diseases (Old Cases) Act 1975, reduced earnings allowance, retirement allowance, severe disablement allowance, sickness benefit, statutory sick pay and unemployment benefits.

Certain payments are exempt. These include: 'small payments', ie those not exceeding £2,500, payments under s 35 of the Powers of the Criminal Courts Act, damages awarded under the Fatal Accidents Act 1976, awards of criminal injury compensation, certain payments from trusts, payments under accident insurance policies and redundancy payments.

In *Hassall v Secretary of State for Social Security* (1994), the applicants were unemployed at the time of the accident and in receipt of benefits. Each received approximately the same amount of benefit as before but on a different basis as they were then incapable of working. There claims were settled on the basis of no loss of earnings, as even if they had been fit for work, they would not have found any. Their benefits were recouped by the Secretary of State, as they were paid 'in consequence of the accident'. These recoupable benefits had replaced non-recoupable benefits they had received previously and the applicants were consequently under-compensated. It was held by the Court of Appeal that loss of non-recoupable benefit should have been claimed as damages by the applicants against the tortfeasor.

Private insurance payments are not deducted since the defendant would therefore profit from the plaintiff's foresight. Payments made under an accident insurance policy taken out by an employer on behalf of employees is also non deductible (*McCamley v Cammell Laird Shipbuilders Ltd* (1990)). *Ex gratia* payments made by a charity are also not deductible. An occupational disability pension is not deducted (*Parry v Cleaver* (1970)). This was affirmed in *Smoker v London Fire and Civil Defence Authority* (1991) on the basis that a pension is deferred payment. Occupational sick pay will be deducted (*Hussain v New Taplow Paper Mills Ltd* (1988)).

In *Longdon v British Coal Corporation* (1995), the plaintiff was allowed to recover loss of earnings, while receiving incapacity pension to which he had contributed. The payments resulted from the plaintiff's prudence and insurance against an incapacitating accident.

Pain and suffering

The plaintiff is entitled to be compensated for actual and prospective pain and suffering. Section 1(1)(6) of the Administration of Justice Act 1982 allows a plaintiff who knows that his life expectancy has been reduced to recover for that anguish. A permanently unconscious plaintiff cannot claim for pain and suffering (*Wise v Kaye* (1962)).

Loss of faculty and amenity

A tariff system of £X for the loss of a leg and £Y for the loss of an arm exists. Refer to Kemp and Kemp for details. Loss of amenity involves the lost chances to use the faculty. Loss of amenity will be greater for a keen sportsman that loses a leg than a couch potato who spends his life watching television.

The award of loss of amenity is made objectively, it was held in *H West & Sons Ltd v Shephard* (1964), where the plaintiff was unconscious and unable to appreciate his condition.

The Law Commission in its Consultation Paper No 140 provisionally favours the continuation of damages for non-pecuniary loss. It also rejects the idea that a threshold for the recovery of non-pecuniary loss should be introduced.

New methods of paying damages in personal injury cases

Structured settlements

For many years, damages were assessed once and paid in one lump sum payment. The rule that damages are assessed once still applies but since the case of *Kelly v Dawes* (1989) payments can be made in the form of periodic payments known as structured settlements. These were first introduced in the US and Canada, where they are further advanced. Their inception in this country was made possible by the Inland Revenue agreeing that periodic payments were payment of capital and not income which had certain tax advantages.

The system works with the lump sum being calculated in the conventional way. Part of the lump sum is paid over to the plaintiff immediately. The rest of the payment is used to purchase an annuity from an insurer with payments being structured over a given period which can be for the plaintiff's lifetime or longer if the plaintiff has dependants.

Advantages of structured settlements

The main advantage is that the periodic payments are free of tax in the plaintiff's hands. The payments are treated by the Inland Revenue as an 'antecedent debt' and are therefore treated as capital rather than income and are not subject to income tax. Contrast this with the investment income from a lump sum which is subject to income tax.

There are also financial advantages for the defendant's insurer. As structures involve the insurer in greater administration costs and they also argue that they are entitled to a share of the resulting tax benefits to the plaintiff, they are able to negotiate a discount on the lump sum, which is usually between the range of 8–15%. It has been argued that a discount in excess of 8% makes structured settlements unattractive as they are likely to be out performed by investments. This view has been criticised on the grounds that it overlooks the value of the certainty the plaintiff has in knowing that his periodic payments are secure. They are useful in cases where the plaintiff would be unable to manage a lump sum payment. They also lead to the plaintiff escaping management and investment costs of investing a lump sum. The income derived from the annuity is protected from the vagaries of the inflation rate or wild fluctuations in the stock market.

There is flexibility in the creation of the structure. The parties can decide the proportion of the lump sum payment that is to go into an immediate capital payment and how much is to go into the structure. They ensure that the payments will not cease during the plaintiff's lifetime. A lump sum payment can be dissipated by the plaintiff either through being spendthrift or through ill advised investment or because a prognosis as to life expectancy proves to be incorrect with the plaintiff living longer than has been anticipated. Regardless of the manner in which the dissipation occurs, the plaintiff will become a charge on the State when it is the aim of the compensation system to avoid this happening.

The Law Commission identified other advantages such as encouraging early settlement, thereby saving time and costs and providing certainty for the plaintiff. Early settlement reduces the stress of the litigation process which has proved to be harmful to the plaintiff's rehabilitation. Where the Law Commission provides the plaintiff with an income they better fulfil the aims of compensation compared to a lump sum payment as they actually substitute what the plaintiff has lost. They provide income in place of lost earnings.

An advantage for the State is that the defendant is much less likely to claim welfare benefit. It also creates less pressure on the legal system as it promotes early settlement of claims and it ensures that the compensation is used for the purpose for which it is intended. Early settlement improves the image of the compensation system. Instead of the insurer handing over a lump sum to the plaintiff and washing his hands entirely of the case, the replacement system ensures provision is made for the rest of the plaintiff's life. In this sense, it is a more humane system.

Disadvantages of structured settlements

As the amount of the structure is only assessed once the problem of guesswork involved in the assessment of damages is not solved. The Law Commission in their Consultation Paper said 'the pressure to get it right at an early stage is extreme'. It is still possible for the amount of damages to prove inadequate due to an incorrect prognosis. The Pearson Commission recommended a system of structured settlements which would be reviewed in the light of deteriorating financial circumstances which would circumvent some of the problems relating to guesswork, but the proposal has not been adopted. To a certain extent all compensatory systems are subject to a certain amount of guesswork. Even a fully reviewable system of periodic payments still has to be based on assumptions relating to promotion prospects, etc.

A further disadvantage is that the operation of the structure is not very flexible. Once the structure is established it cannot be changed. If there is unforeseen demand for capital, the structure will not be able to accommodate this need. This contrasts with the degree of flexibility which exists at the time the structure is created when the parties can decide how much will be given in immediate capital payment and how much will go into the structure. For a minority of plaintiffs, the loss of freedom and discretion as to the manner in which the lump sum should be invested is a serious disadvantage.

The plaintiff is also subject to the risk that the insurer may become insolvent. Although there are attempts made to protect the plaintiff against this contingency, there is no guarantee that the plaintiff is immune from this risk.

The system may simply replace 'compensation neurosis' with a different form of neurosis. The plaintiff may perceive his dependency on the monthly cheque as making his position analogous to a welfare recipient. The system also increases administrative costs and imposes a long-term financial obligation on the defendant.

If the question is looked at in its wider context, then it can be seen that as tort victims are already generously compensated in comparison to those who receive compensation outside the tort system then the system in the words of Michael Jones in *Textbook on Torts* makes an 'elite group even more elite'.

Structured settlements do not alter the fact that the system is predicated on compensating the plaintiff for what he has lost rather than on what he needs. By alleviating some of the difficulties associated with the lump sum system, structured settlements may simply be postponing a more fundamental reform of the compensation system.

Limits to structured settlements

Structures cannot be used in all cases and certain limits have been placed upon them:

- Both parties must consent to the structure. It was held in *Burke v Tower Hamlets AHA* (1989) that the defendant could not be made to make periodic payments against its wishes. The Law Commission in its Report, 'Structured Settlements and Interim and Provisional Damages' (No 224) recommended that courts should not have the power to impose settlements.
- A structure cannot be imposed after the parties have formally agreed settlement or obtained judgment for a certain sum.
- A structure cannot be imposed where provisional damages are sought nor where interim damages have been awarded.
- It cannot be used in very small claims as administrative costs make it uneconomic.
- They cannot be used where there is no liability, eg awards made by the Criminal Injuries Compensation Board (CICB), despite their decisions being subject to judicial review.

The Law Commission in its Report No 224 recommends that the CICB should be put into a position where it can purchase annuities. It is also unclear whether the Motor Insurers' Bureau (MIB), which also awards *ex gratia* payments can be a party to a structured settlement. Again the Law Commission recommends that they be empowered to offer structured settlements. So far structures have only been awarded in cases of personal injury and it is doubtful whether they will be extended into other areas.

Structures are not available for special damages but are reserved specifically for general damages, ie those damages which cannot be calculated precisely, including future loss.

A more subtle limitation on structured settlements relates to situations where the tax situation prejudices the insurer's clash flow. The defendant's insurer purchases an annuity from a life insurer. The life insurer has to pay tax on the annuity payments it makes to the defendant's insurer, which grosses up the payments it makes to the plaintiff. The defendant's insurer has to wait 12–18 months before it can claim back the tax, usually by way of offsetting the payments against its Corporation Tax, with obvious implications for cash flow. The Law Commission has asked for comment as to whether this constitutes a disincentive to insurers to become involved in structured settlements. Their provisional view is that it does not. However, certain insurers such as mutual insurers have no opportunity to offset the cost of grossing up against tax liability and therefore do not get involved in structured settlements.

Provisional damages

One solution to the problem of guesswork in the assessment of damages is provisional damages. Established by s 6 of the Administration of Justice Act 1982 which amends s 32(a) of the Supreme Court Act 1981. They enable the plaintiff in personal injury cases, where there is a 'chance' that, as a result of the tort, the plaintiff will develop some serious deterioration in his condition, to be awarded provisional damages assessed on the basis that the disease or deterioration will not occur. This can help alleviate the stress on a plaintiff who is worried that his compensation will prove inadequate in the event of his injuries being worse than expected.

However, the procedure is only rarely used. The first award of provisional damages must be made by court order. The parties thereby lose the advantages which arise from a private settlement of the case. There have been problems over the definition of 'chance' of a 'serious deterioration'. In *Willson v Ministry of Defence* (1991), the development of arthritis after an ankle injury was held to be a progression of a particular disease and not a 'chance event'. Scott Baker J said that there had to be 'a clear and severable risk rather than a continuing deterioration'. Further disadvantages are that the plaintiff is only allowed one further chance of a review of his damages and in practice the plaintiff must ask for less damages than he would otherwise be entitled to since the provisional award ignores the fact that a deterioration can occur.

The Law Commission is considering reforms to the system of provisional damages but has initially said in its Consultation Paper that few reforms are needed. The drawbacks mean that the system has not been widely used and has mainly been used in cases where there is a chance of epilepsy or there has been exposure to asbestos.

Split trials and interim damages

Split trials and interim damages mean that there can be separate trials on liability and *quantum* of damages. This is permitted by Ord 33 r 4 of the Rules of the Supreme Court. It is an exception to the finality of litigation principle since it allows two actions. Order 29 r 11 of the Rules of the Supreme Court allow an interim award of damages to be made to the plaintiff pending the outcome of the *quantum* portion of the trial, where the plaintiff shows need. The advantage of the system is that the question of *quantum* can be settled at a later date when the plaintiff's prognosis is clearer and can, therefore, be more accurately assessed.

The disadvantage of the system is that it adds to delay in the final settlement of cases. Delay is already a feature of the compensation system that attracts a considerable amount of criticism. They are also treated with a certain amount of distrust by defendants who fear that the delay will enable the plaintiff to set up an expensive care programme.

Damage to property

Where property is completely destroyed, the measure of damages is the market value of the property at the time of destruction.

In *Liesbosch Dredger v SS Edison* (1933), the plaintiffs were unable to recover where they had incurred additional expenses since they were too impecunious to hire an alternative vessel while theirs was being repaired.

More recently, hire costs have been allowed in *Martindale v Duncan* (1973). In *Motorworks Ltd v Alwahabi* (1977), it was reasonable for the plaintiff to hire a Rolls Royce, while his own Rolls Royce was being repaired.

Where property is damaged but not destroyed, the measure of damages is the diminution in value, normally the cost of repair.

Mitigation of loss

A plaintiff has a duty to mitigate the damage that results from the defendant's tort. But no wrong is committed against the defendant if he fails to do so. In *Darbishire v Warran* (1963), it was said that the plaintiff is 'entitled to be as extravagant as he pleases but not at the expense of the defendant'.

Injunctions

An injunction is an equitable remedy and is therefore, discretionary. A prohibitory injunction is an order of the court requiring the defendant to cease committing a continuing tort. As an equitable remedy, it will not be awarded if damages would be an adequate remedy.

Mandatory injunctions are not granted so readily as prohibitory injunctions; there must be a strong probability that very serious damage to the plaintiff will result if withheld.

Death in relation to tort

Death can extinguish liability for tort and it may also, in certain circumstances, create liability in tort.

Death as extinguishing liability

At common law, the general rule was that death of either party extinguished any existing cause of action by one against the other. Actions in contract and instances where the deceased appropriated the property to his estate escaped this rule.

As a result of this rule, if a negligent driver was killed in an accident which had been caused by his own negligence, then nothing could be recovered from his estate or from his insurer. The Law Reform (Miscellaneous Provisions) Act 1934 was passed to provide for the survival of the causes of action.

Survival of causes of action

Section 1(1) provides that all causes of action subsisting against or vested in any person on his death, except causes of action for defamation, now survive against, or, as the case may be, for the benefit of, his estate.

It is not possible to defame the dead but there have been recommendations that there should be a right of action for five years after a person dies which would be available to close relations.

'Subsisting' action

The Law Reform (Miscellaneous Provisions) Act 1934 specifies that the right of action must be 'subsisting', sometimes the wrongdoer may have died before a cause of action has accrued, eg a manufacturer may have died before his product has actually caused damage.

Section 1(4) provides where damage has been suffered as a result of a wrongful act in respect of which a cause of action would have subsisted had the wrongdoer not died before or at the same time as the damage was suffered, there shall be deemed to have subsisted against him before his death such cause of action as would have subsisted if he had died after the damage had been suffered.

Damages recoverable

Where the injured party dies, the damages recoverable for the benefit of the estate may not include exemplary damages, nor any damages for loss of income for any period after the victim's death.

The latter is concerned with the 'lost years' whereby a victim can claim for loss of earnings during a period during which he could have been expected to live had he not had his life expectancy reduced by the defendant. The 'lost years' are not recoverable when the defendant is dead. The reason lies behind the relationship between the Law Reform (Miscellaneous Provisions) Act 1934 and the Fatal Accidents Act 1976.

- If a dead defendant was liable for the 'lost years' then he would be doubly liable as he would have to compensate dependants for the same thing under the Fatal Accidents Act 1976.
- If the injured person died as a result of the accident in respect of which his dependents or his estate are claiming, then the damage must be calculated without reference to any loss or gain to the deceased's estate except funeral expenses.
- If the deceased's death is unconnected with the incident which gave rise to the cause of action, substantial damages can be recovered even in situations where the deceased, had he been alive, would only have been entitled to nominal damages.
- Death terminates losses such as pain and suffering and loss of amenity.
- Damages recovered on behalf of a deceased form part of his estate and can be used to pay off his debts and be given as legacies.

The Law Reform (Contributory Negligence) Act 1945 applies to claims by estates, as does the law of limitations to claims by or against estates. When the tortfeasor dies, the ordinary measure of damages will apply.

Death as creating liability

The Law Reform (Miscellaneous Provisions) Act 1934 allowed actions to continue against deceased persons and also allowed for the continuance of claims by deceased persons.

Another rule of the common law said that death did not give rise to a cause of action in other persons even though they may have been dependent on the deceased.

It was said by Lord Ellenborough in *Baker v Bolton* (1808) that 'the death of a human being could not be complained of as an injury'.

Fatal Accidents Act 1976

Initially, the Fatal Accidents Act 1846 overturned the common law as far as dependents who were specified in the Act and in later legislation were concerned.

The Fatal Accidents Act 1976 consolidates earlier legislation. The 1976 Act provides that whenever the death of a person is caused by the wrongful act, neglect or default of another such as would have entitled the injured person who would have been liable if death had not ensued shall be liable to an action for damages on behalf of the dependants.

Dependants

Section 1 of the Fatal Accidents Act 1976 was amended by the Administration of Justice Act 1982 the class now includes:

- a spouse or former spouse of the deceased, or person who was living as the spouse of the deceased, in the same household, immediately before the date of the death and had been so living for at least two years;
- any parent or other ascendant of the deceased or person treated by the deceased as his parent;
- any child or other descendant of the deceased or any person who has been treated as a child of the family in relation to any marriage of the deceased;
- any person who is, or is the issue of a brother, sister, uncle or aunt of the deceased.

An adopted person is a child of the persons by whom he or she was adopted, a half blood relation is treated as a full relation. A step-child of any person is treated as the step-parents' child and an illegitimate person is treated as the legitimate child of the mother and reputed father.

An action under the Fatal Accidents Act 1976 must normally be brought on behalf of the dependants by his executor or administrator of the deceased but where there is no personal representative any dependant entitled to sue under the Act may sue in his own name and on behalf of other dependants. An action must be brought within three years.

Nature of the action
Rights of action under the Fatal Accidents Act 1976 is a new cause of action, separate from the deceased's cause of action. There is no claim if the deceased's action is statute barred at the date of his death.

Under the Law Reform (Contributory Negligence) Act 1948 if the deceased was partly to blame for the accident the dependant's damages will be reduced accordingly.

What is recoverable
In respect of death after 1982, the spouse of the deceased or the parents of a minor who never married may claim a fixed sum of £7,500 for 'bereavement'.

The wide class of dependants may claim damages for loss of support. The damages must be proportioned to the injury. The Act lays down no principle for assessing damage. The test normally used is *Franklin v SE Ry* (1858), damages must be calculated *per* Pollock CB 'in reference to a reasonable expectation of pecuniary benefit as of right, or otherwise, from the continuance of the life'. Thus, if the dependants have only suffered nominal damage, no damages will be recoverable. Loss of a mother's care is held to be a pecuniary benefit.

A son who was killed but had worked for his father for full wages, did not entitle the father to a claim, as these had been properly paid but a father was entitled to a claim under the Act when the son had voluntarily assisted him in the business.

There will also be a claim where there is reasonable probability that a person, likely in the near future to earn a substantial wage, and thereby support dependants, is killed. This will not apply if there is a possibility of someone supporting the claimant in the near future.

Assessment of damages
Damages for bereavement are a fixed sum owed to a narrow class of persons. Other damages are assessed on a pecuniary loss basis. Each dependent's pecuniary loss will be separately assessed. The process of assessment is very similar to personal injury assessment. The court

determines the net annual loss and then works out a multiplier. The deceased's net annual income will be reduced to allow for a portion of income which would have been spent entirely on himself. Benefits which have accrued to the deceased's estate since his death are disregarded.

It was held in *Hunter v Butler* (1995) that there is no loss of dependency under the Fatal Accidents Act 1976 in respect of undeclared earnings, otherwise known as 'moonlighting' or for loss of housing benefit and supplementary benefit.

Index